EMULATION AND INVENTION

EMULATION
AND INVENTION

BY

Brooke Hindle

NEW YORK

NEW YORK UNIVERSITY PRESS

1981

Library of Congress Cataloging in Publication Data

Hindle, Brooke.
  Emulation and invention.

  (The Anson G. Phelps lectureship series on early
American history)
  Bibliography: p.
  Includes index.
  1. Technology—United States—History. 2. Steamboats
—United States—History. 3. Telegraph—United States
—History. I. Title. II. Series: New York University.
Stokes Foundation. Anson G. Phelps lectureship on early
American history.
T21.H49   621'.0973   80-29438
ISBN 0-8147-3409-X

CONTENTS

For
Margee and Bob
Sally and Don

PREFACE

THE INVENTIVENESS and creativity at the center of mechanical technology are the concern of this book. Most central is the question of the mental manipulation of images and ideas that always precedes the trial and construction and even the repair and modification of machines. A secondary concern is the nature of the American environment that encouraged inventiveness in certain lines of mechanical endeavor and permitted the Americans, despite their distance from the European centers of wealth and industrial leadership, to pioneer in certain innovations.

The steamboat and the telegraph are used as case studies because they, more than the sweeping technological change occurring in textile production, machine tool development, iron reduction, or farm mechanization, represented conceptually new technologies. The steamboat had been impossible before the steam engine and the telegraph impracticable before knowledge of electromagnetism. The introduction of the long train of developments in powered transportation and in instantaneous electrical communication represented major technological change, the beginning points of which are more identifiable than in most sequences of modification.

Also, the development of the steamboat and the telegraph is notable for the prominence of artists among the projectors. The fine arts and the mechanic arts had already diverged so much that this was a matter for comment by contemporaries. Today, the explanation seems intimately related to the mode of thought required in mechanical technology.

This book, then, is an essay on the mode of thinking behind

important technological innovations of the early nineteenth century. Conventional annotation is included in order not to blur specifics, but it does not identify a research report. This is an essay on mechanical technology.

The thinking presented here is a product of several years of study and contemplation of the ways of technology, sharpened by my experiences in the National Museum of American History, of the Smithsonian Institution. I owe much to individual curators and specialists and to others within the Smithsonian for information, photographs, and ideas. A debt more difficult to specify is to the pervasive sense within the museum of the inner nature of the technological enterprise and of material culture. This emphasizes the conviction that surviving artifacts, drawings, and photographs provide an entry to the understanding of technology not attainable from the written record alone.

Particular help was received from Jon B. Eklund, curator of chemistry; Bernard S. Finn, curator of electricity; Elizabeth Harris, curator of graphic arts; Howard Hoffman, museum specialist; Margaret B. Klapthor, curator of civil history; James A. Knowles, museum specialist; Gary Kulik, curator of textile technology; Philip K. Lundeberg, curator of naval history; Robert P. Multhauf, senior historian; Robert Vogel, curator of mechanical and civil engineering; and John H. White, curator of railroads. Among those in other Smithsonian bureaus who helped specifically were: Silvio A. Bedini, rare book librarian; Beverly J. Cox, curator at the National Portrait Gallery; William R. Massa, Jr., technician at the Smithsonian Archives; and Nathan Reingold, editor of the Joseph Henry Papers.

Elsewhere in the Washington area, the published and manuscript sources for this study are richer than in any other city. The Library of Congress, the National Archives, and the Patent Office are the primary repositories.

Fundamental sources and inspiration were found at almost every center along the Washington-Boston corridor, always rendered through helpful individuals, only a few of whom can be named. In Baltimore, important materials are held by the Papers of Benjamin Henry Latrobe and at the Maryland Historical Society, and in Wilmington at the Eleutherian Mills Historical Library and the Hagley Museum—there the insights of Eugene S. Ferguson and David A. Hounshell were important. In Philadelphia, the American Philosophical Society, the Library Company of Philadelphia, and the Historical Society of Pennsylvania made available unique materials. In New Brunswick, the resource was Reese V. Jenkins, editor of the Papers of Thomas A. Edison. In Newark, at the New Jersey Historical Society, Alan D. Frazer provided ideas and materials. In New York, great sources were found at the New-York Historical Society, the New York Public Library, and at New York University, where critical knowledge was offered by Bayrd Still, archivist of the university. In the Boston area, the major holdings are at the Boston Public Library and the Harvard College Library. In ideas, the contributions of Cyril S. Smith, professor emeritus at Massachusetts Institute of Technology, and Samuel Y. Edgerton, then professor at Boston University, were valuable. Across the sea, in London, the British Library and the Science Museum lent aid.

The illustrations are an integral part of this book which emphasizes spatial or nonverbal thinking. Photographs of artifacts, drawings, paintings, and prints were provided, and permission to use them extended by a large number of institutions, including the American Philosophical Society, the American Society of Mechanical Engineers, the Art Committee of the City of New York, the Birmingham Public Libraries, the Corcoran Gallery of Art, the Historical Society of Pennsylvania, the Library of Congress, the Maryland Historical Society, the Metropolitan Museum of Art, the National Academy of Design, the New-York Historical Society, the William R. Nelson Gallery of Art, the Ohio Historical Society, the Papers of Benjamin Henry Latrobe, the Science Museum in London, England, the University of Michigan, and the Yale University Art Gallery. The largest number of photographs came from the Smithsonian Institution: from the National Portrait Gallery and the Smithsonian Institution Archives, but dominantly from the National Museum of American History. Joseph L. Kennedy and the staff of the Office of Printing and Photographic Services in the Smithsonian Institution are responsible for the photography behind over a third of the illustrations.

The Anson G. Phelps lectureship at New York University

provided the occasion for thinking through and writing the present book. Carl E. Prince, chairman of the History Department, and Frederick C. Schult, Jr., chairman of the lecture committee, helped at all the difficult points. At the New York University Press, Malcolm C. Johnson, Jr., and Robert L. Bull were uniformly supportive, and Despina Papazoglou has been dynamically helpful. James L. Mairs of W. W. Norton has been responsive throughout. The opportunity to carry through this study has been made available by the Smithsonian Institution.

Rosemary Regan typed the manuscript several times, not only skillfully but sometimes with creative intervention. My wife, Helen, shared at every stage—search and research, thought and reformulation—in the pain and joy of developing the book.

LIST OF ILLUSTRATIONS

The Machine
in the New Nation

THE MEN who made the American Revolution were supremely conscious of their role in history. In bringing forth a new nation, they expressed an accumulated sense of destiny that embraced the hopes and convictions of generations who had labored and fought for a new start. Within the Revolution, they produced a new ideology, compounded of the republicanism they had imported from across the sea and the republicanism they had lived within their own nearly self-governing provinces. In resounding phrases, they announced a faith in progress and material betterment in a society that encouraged the individual to his noblest effort.

The American Revolutionaries never heard the expression "Industrial Revolution," but they had a growing sense of the changes later described in that rather flawed term. As they became increasingly conscious of the vast scope of desirable "American improvement" and the seemingly feeble means at hand for attaining it, they could not fail to notice the new technological capabilities developing within Great Britain. By the time they launched their experiment in independence, some had caught the infectious enthusiasm for mechanization.

The American Revolution and the Industrial Revolution overlapped remarkably in time, although no specific span of years yields defensible truth about either. Both of the movements had deep and tangled roots, and the two were held largely to separated courses during the American War for

Independence. Some of their peaks, however, coincided in a curious way. The year 1776, for example, became for the American commonwealth the most celebrated of all dates, the year in which independence was proclaimed. It was also a year of two important peaks in the Industrial Revolution. James Watt gave his first public demonstration of his first commercial model of the condensing steam engine on March 8, 1776, offering the world the cheap power source that would dominate industrial development for the next century. Two days later, Adam Smith's *Wealth of Nations* made its first appearance in the London bookstores, a work that would condition American as much as British attitudes through the same century.[1]

Later generations of Americans continued to celebrate their Revolution as a "new birth of freedom" that had set the stage for the remarkable American saga of growth, of the broadening of political power, and of individual liberty. They did not similarly celebrate the Industrial Revolution, although what the United States has become rests heavily upon it and upon the manner in which the Americans applied and improved its technology to develop their wonderful resources of people, land, waters, trees, and minerals. The newly opened door to "virtue, liberty, and independence" was celebrated throughout the country at periodic intervals; the newly opened door to riches for all through mechanization was hardly celebrated at all. Some contemporaries, however, did perceive that widening aperture, struggled to move through it, and dreamed great dreams of what might lie beyond.

Of course the British did not know what lay beyond either, so they, earlier than the Americans, were responsive to those who offered guidance on how to encourage the most beneficial mechanization. Adam Smith placed mechanization next to the division of labor in his analysis. "Everybody," he asserted, "must be sensible how much labour is facilitated and abridged by the proper application of machinery." His formula for encouraging inventiveness and mechanical innovation had the advantage of simplicity and conformity with familiar currents of Enlightenment ideology. Mechanization could be applied to improve life most surely if each individual would just follow his own economic self-interest. The "invisible hand" would then combine the multiple forces of the marketplace to the end of "universal opulence which extends itself to the lowest ranks of people."[2]

The miracle was that, especially for the Americans, it worked. The new nation was born just in time to receive, install, and improve upon the applicable technologies developing in Britain. Each of four areas of technological development within the Industrial Revolution excited American avidity in different measure. England's coal-fuel technology had the least immediate appeal, especially as applied to iron production. The newly mechanized textile production, however, had evident economic advantages, especially in this undeveloped country, but it was not quickly coupled to steampower because of the abundance of our waterpower sites. The steam engine instead was used most dramatically in new forms of transportation, but at the same time it spread less visibly to a variety of manufacturing applications. Textile machinery and steam engines required the rapid development of machine tools and machining capabilities—the fourth leg of the Industrial Revolution. Incredibly, the newborn United States was more successful than any other nation in assuming the attitude of mind required and in transferring any desired technology.

How could that possibly be? How could a thinly dispersed people, 90 percent of them engaged in agricultural pursuits, a people whose economy was still colonial and commercial, take over the most advanced technology in the world? More amazing still, how could the custodians of an empty continent, far distant from the economic power centers of Europe and from its busy workshops and rising factories, move on to take leadership in one line after another of mechanization and innovation?

The answers are many, but two of the most important have been hidden by myths. One is the myth that the United States began in 1776—or at best that its history stretches back no further than 1607. Against this sense of things, colonial historians have long struggled with only partial success. In fact, the United States shares the history of the West, not only before 1607, but since then—even to the present day. Independence did not establish an isolated political and social organism; it merely ended the political control Great Britain had exercised. The economic fabric, the cultural and institutional fabrics had to be rewoven somewhat, but many more interlacing threads were regularly added than those which had to be severed. Especially in introducing the new technology and its organizational framework, the United States drew continuously upon the strengths of Europe.

The second obscuring myth is the myth of the pastoral, bucolic innocence of colonial society—an innocence especially of machines and mechanization.[3] If most of the people were farmers, then it is easily assumed that machines must have been alien to them. A country with only a few commercial, provincial cities—none so large as a twelfth the size of London—must have depended upon simple handtools, upon what in another distortion is tagged traditional or preindustrial technology. If this view of American technology had been true, the assimilation of Britain's new mechanisms never could have happened as fast as it did, because machine technology can be transferred, adapted, and kept in operation only by mechanics who through long intimacy with mechanical devices are able to sense and feel the motions of a machine, almost to think like a machine.

The fallacy lies in the assumption that colonial Americans were unfamiliar with machines. In actuality, the Americans—particularly the farmers—lived daily with machines, and a small group of mechanics and artisans worked daily with gears and gear trains, cams, ratchets, escapements, bearings, cylinders, pistons, valves, and cocks—the basic elements of which the new machinery was constructed. Moreover, the machinery the farmer knew—the seed drill, the turpentine and whiskey stills, the gristmills and sawmills, and the clock—were eminently comprehensible to all who worked with them. Colonials were often more familiar with the ways of the machine than the city dweller of the present who, confronted at every turn with a "black-box" technology, sometimes knows no more of the principles of mechanism involved than the young child who learns "on" and "off" among his earliest words.

The transfer of technology to America began in the initial settlements at a time when England itself was struggling to assimilate technologies developed on the Continent. Then and throughout the colonial period the primary means for transferring a new technology was to bring in a group of skilled operatives familiar with the mechanisms involved. Thus did England strengthen its own industrial base, which was relatively undeveloped as late as 1500. In the sixteenth and seventeenth centuries, German miners, Flemish weavers, and French glassworkers and horologists transferred to England technologies that grew and prospered. In the same pattern, Italian silk reelers, Dutch and Polish glassworkers, and German sawyers were sent to Jamestown.[4]

This reliance on "fingertip knowledge" rather than on books, drawings, and written materials was inescapable, but a new category of books offered a supplementary way to transfer and diffuse technology. The explosion of the printed word in the fifteenth century had been paralleled by developments in art that for the first time made it possible to represent three-dimensional machines accurately and understandably. The new graphics made use of linear perspective, the exploded view, the cutaway view, and chiaroscuro—or light and shade.[5] These techniques were first applied to surveys of practice or manuals, the best known of which is Agricola's on mining.[6] Then they were seized upon by a group of Italian, French, and German artist-engineers of the sixteenth and seventeenth centuries to produce a wonderful group of "theaters of machines," as several of the books were entitled. From Jacques Besson in 1569 and Agostino Ramelli in 1588 to Jacob Leupold in 1724–39, these celebratory volumes were produced in exaltation of the capabilities of the machine, often for court patrons.[7] They reduced to two-dimensional form the grand constructions that could not be placed beside the instruments in a *Kunstkammer*, and they had some of the éclat attached to the paintings and sculpture produced similarly for the courts.

Even when the more literate English mechanic was aware of the virtuoso performances represented in the theaters of machines, he usually did not have access to them. The books were published on the Continent in vernacular languages and translated from one language to another, but none of the general machine books was translated in its own day into

English. James Watt, recognizing that Leupold's information on the steam engine and related machinery might be important in his own work, actually learned German in order to be able to read the book.[8]

England's failure to produce her own theaters of machines initially reflected a generally backward technology. Even in printing, England lagged grievously, having in 1500 only thirteen presses, against over a thousand on the Continent.[9] Moreover, England was a sea power and did not produce the kind of engineer who on the Continent began the sequence of theaters of machines. In time, England's printing capabilities grew, and by the eighteenth century she attained leadership in several fields of technology, including navigational and mathematical instruments, clockmaking, and gunnery, as well as in a series of coal-fuel industries—but when she reached a position to produce fine machine books, she did not. Instead, the English published manuals for the mechanic, often brief and inexpensive but illustrated; dictionaries of arts and sciences, illustrated with good copperplate engravings; and general encyclopedias.

England's technological advance was certainly uneven, but most of the machine technologies that crossed the Atlantic were generically common to England and the Continent. Some were initially transferred by Continental artisans sent from mother countries to their own colonies, as by the Dutch to the Hudson and by the Swedes to the Delaware. Non-English immigrants to the English colonies also transferred Continental versions of certain technologies—the Germans, especially in Pennsylvania, and the French at several seaboard points. Yet most technology was transferred by English, Scottish, and Irish artisans. The leading cities—Philadelphia, Boston, and New York—received a continuing stream of artisans, most of them from London, quickly making available the skills and newer developments of the British metropolis.[10]

The largest and most visible machines in the American landscape were gristmills and iron furnaces and forges, necessarily located at waterpower sites. Water mills were almost uniformly powered by vertical wheels, most of them undershot; windmills were used less frequently. Both water- and windmills used similar wooden gearing, depending nearly always upon crown and lantern gears to make the 90-degree turn. Furnaces that used a blast depended upon water-powered bellows and forges used a powered cam to raise and drop the hammer. Sometimes plating, rolling, and slitting mills pounded the iron into sheets that were slit into rods for nails.[11]

Many smaller machines were also well known. Firearms, mostly muskets, were repaired and manufactured here, and the Pennsylvania rifle evolved from the German prototype into a very accurate weapon during the colonial period. Water pumps, both lift pumps and force pumps, as they were then known, were widely used for raising water, in fire engines, and aboard ships. The clock represented a metaphor of mechanization; it was fully automatic, having only to be wound and set. Some clocks played tunes, displayed the phases of the moon, and presented the date. Clockmakers used machine tools such as grindstones, lathes, and clockmakers' engines, and the best of them also made transits and theodolites. David Rittenhouse's unique orreries or mechanical planetaria were more encouraged in the English-speaking world than the elaborate automata that equally expressed machine enthusiasm on the Continent.[12]

In rare instances, the Americans received examples of machine technology that were unusual in the English scene. A remarkable example of this was the installation in 1754 at the Moravian German town of Bethlehem, Pennsylvania, of a pumped and piped water supply system that brought running water into the houses and shops. There was nothing new about the system or its elements. It was based upon an eighteen-foot undershot waterwheel; bored log conduits; a central reservoir; and, after 1762, three piston pumps. Such systems were frequent on the Continent, although in Britain even London lagged in keeping up with its water supply needs. The Americans did not take up the Bethlehem example, and our largest cities encountered aggravated water problems before we even began to apply the available technology. The failure was not technological but social; emphasis upon private enterprise rendered large public works of this sort difficult—here as in Britain.[13]

The sawmill was another example of Continental machine

technology that was widely applied throughout the colonies but not in Britain. Like the gristmill, the sawmill was used in every colony and relied upon as a necessity. It was first brought to America in 1611 by a group of artisans from Hamburg, engaged for the purpose by the Virginia Company. Most of the structures in America were clad with sawed weatherboard; ships, boats, and wagons also depended upon sawed timber. Not to have adopted the sawmill in America would have been to slow development seriously and to impoverish society.[14]

Yet England had no sawmills—none; the contrast is incredible. Sawmills had been clearly pictured and described in a number of the theaters of machines, and in 1663 a Dutchman erected one in England, where worker antagonism was so strong that it was soon abandoned. A century later a mob pulled down another attempted sawmill, although this time those responsible were prosecuted and sawmills were assured of protection. Yet they made no headway, and nineteenth-century American visitors were amazed to see almost nothing but handsawing.[15] The usual explanation of this phenomenon, as an expression of antagonism to mechanization by workers who feared for their jobs, places the incidents within a long catalogue of English machine breaking. It is, however, an insufficient explanation. The deeper cause was England's depletion of wood, which had become serious as early as the thirteenth century and which had had a great impact upon her technology.

Paralleling those technologies which were not developed in England but became a part of the American scene were examples of technologies of the greatest importance in England that were not transferred or were of only slight importance in America. The most conspicuous of these were also caused by the differential in wood supply. Fundamental was a complex of coal-based technologies that wholly transformed many industries and laid the foundation for the Industrial Revolution of the eighteenth century. Indeed, the conversion to coal has been called "the first industrial revolution."[16]

Beginning in the fourteenth century, but accelerating especially in the sixteenth and seventeenth centuries, England led the world out of the wooden age and into a new reliance upon coal. She moved in this direction solely out of necessity—because she ran out of wood long before France and the economically active areas of northern Europe. Much of England's rising coal trade was directed toward supplying domestic hearths, but from an early time coal was used industrially, first by blacksmiths and armorers, and then by gunsmiths, pewterers, and coppersmiths. When applied to salt production through the evaporation of sea water, it gave England virtual self-sufficiency in that increasingly necessary preservative. Lime burning, textile finishing, saltpeter, alum, gunpowder, soap, and sugar all yielded to coal. Yet coal almost always altered the industrial processes to which it was applied; it could not be used as wood was because of its polluting character. By protecting the product from direct exposure to coal and its combustion products, the reverberatory furnace solved that problem and made even the production of glass possible. Although iron production had still not yielded to coal, by 1700 England had largely solved its fuel problem and in the process was gaining mastery of a new technological base for her industry. Her industrial production had long since passed that of France, and she may already have gained an unsurpassable lead in the race for mechanization.[17]

But iron was the most essential element in the emerging industrial world, and its production had to be solved. Abraham Darby's limited success in 1709 with coke smelting was only a start. The process did not work with all coke, and under the best circumstances the product was distinctly inferior to charcoal iron. Not until Henry Cort's rolling and puddling patents of 1784 could coke iron be converted economically to wrought iron, and only then did rapid conversion to coal follow. The last gap in the coal-fuel technology was finally closed.[18]

Yet the very reasons that required England's conversion to coal required that America not convert. As in England's earliest use of coal, local deposits were sometimes applied in America to blacksmithing and to domestic use, but there was no reason even to consider its industrial application as long as charcoal remained cheaper than coke and the product more usable and more salable. England did everything she could to encourage pig- and bar-iron production in her colonies, valuing the cheapness and superiority of the product for her own uses. As a consequence, America before independence failed almost totally to receive England's most sweeping technological change prior to the Industrial Revolution—her coal-based industrial system.

This extended the technological divergence between the two countries in critical directions, the most important being the development of the steam engine. The steam engine emerged in England to meet a very specific need, the need to pump water out of deep mines that had increasingly been sunk as surface deposits of coal were exhausted. The pumping systems imported from Germany with the rest of the mining technology were simply inadequate to cope with mine water, and the Newcomen steam or atmospheric engine of about 1712 provided a partial answer. This was a piston engine in which steam was not used as an active force but only, upon condensation, to create a vacuum into which atmospheric pressure pushed the piston. It was inefficient, cumbersome, and voracious of fuel, although the fuel cost could easily be borne at a coal mine where it was relatively cheap. The engine's use expanded slowly and was mostly limited to pumping applications.[19]

For obvious reasons, the Newcomen engine had almost no applications in America. Whatever coal was used was taken from bogs or shallow deposits, and iron ore, too, was fairly accessible. Lacking deep mines, the Americans had little reason to go to the expense and trouble of trying to make a Newcomen engine work. Only once before the Revolutionary era did such a reason arise, this to pump out the deep copper mine owned by Philip Schuyler at Belleville, New Jersey. The engine, installed in 1753, worked, but its use did not spread. The next Newcomen engine did not appear for another twenty years when Christopher Colles came over from Ireland to demonstrate a model in Philadelphia in 1773 and to build a full-scale engine in New York in 1775. Installed to provide a better water supply for New York City, that application was ended by the British occupation.[20]

Enthusiasm for mechanization and invention was incorporated at an early stage into America's dreams of national destiny. One of the clearest indications that some Americans had caught this contagion was voiced by Benjamin Franklin in reaction to the Iron Act of 1750, which prohibited the erection of any facilities for manufacturing finished iron goods. Franklin warned Britain that she "should not too much restrain Manufactures in her Colonies," because, he predicted, "the greatest Number of Englishmen will be on this Side of the Water" within a relatively short period. Musing about America's growth in technology as in population, he declared that men who invent "new Trades, Arts or Manufactures, or new Improvements in Husbandry, may be properly called Fathers of their Nation."[21]

Just a few years later, Nathaniel Ames grew exultant: "Huge Mountains of Iron Ore are already discovered; and vast Stores are reserved for future Generations: This Metal, more useful than Gold or Silver, will employ millions of hands, not only to form the martial Sword and peaceful Share alternately; but an Infinity of Utensils improved in the exercise of Art, and Handicraft amongst Men."[22] As the Americans moved on to Revolution and Independence, the visions of the prophets became clearer, and an increasingly important question was how to encourage the fulfillment of their predictions. How could men who invent be called forth? How could that "Infinity of Utensils improved in the exercise of Art" be generated?

These questions had long troubled the Europeans; and the Americans, almost unavoidably, took their guidance from the English—an especially favored source being Francis Bacon. He was early installed as a fixture in the colonial colleges; his works were more quickly acquired by the Library Company of Philadelphia than any of the theaters of machines; and Bacon was frequently appealed to in newspapers and magazines. Thomas Jefferson endorsed Bacon, Newton, and Locke, Voltaire's trinity of secular saints, and carried Bacon's picture with him "wherever he went."[23]

What Bacon described as his first principle was a call for the "commerce between the mind and things."[24] He sought a comprehension of the nonverbal—whether of nature or the ways of the artisan. With great enthusiasm, he projected the need for a natural history of trades, to parallel a natural history of living things. He railed against mere book learning, against the blind study of ancient texts, calling for the direct study of nature and of things. He gave eloquent and effective voice to resentment welling up in the artisan community of his day against unproductive verbalizing.[25]

Bacon's influence upon the early Royal Society was strong, and his demand for experimentation and the collection of data was particularly effective. His approach was more balanced than usually represented; he insisted upon a "double scale or ladder"—"ascending from experiments to the invention of causes, and descending from causes to the invention of new experiments."[26] In that early scientific society, Hooke, Hauksbee, Grew, and particularly Boyle carried out effective experimental studies in the belief that they were executing Bacon's concepts. Bacon's support of useful knowledge was evident in their work and in the early volumes of the *Philosophical Transactions*. Yet it is a mistake to interpret either Bacon or the early Royal Society as applying science to practice. That goal was far distant, and Bacon was actually more concerned in enriching science by studying the trades than, immediately, in basing technology upon science.[27]

Indeed the most diligent searchers through Bacon's works found little that could be applied directly to the encouragement of invention or the improvement of technology. His enthusiasm was great and infectious, but his advice was too general to help the artisan or the entrepreneur, except in the basic truth of his realization that the essence of technology was nonverbal, that the approach was not through words or books.

Adam Smith was more specific in identifying both public policies and individual action that might encourage invention and mechanization. Although insensitive to the rising Industrial Revolution he knew that machines were often helpful but urged that their encouragement be left to marketplace competition. Competition, he asserted, could never hurt either producer or consumer; it would make retailers buy dearer and sell cheaper—to the benefit of all. Wherever mechanization or the division of labor was an advantage, it would be introduced because competition would require it.[28]

Through competition, one might reach to the ennobled efforts it provoked, to emulation. This word, much more in currency then than today, was frequently applied to achievement in art and the arts. Smith felt that "an unrestrained competition" never failed to excite "emulation." "Rivalship and emulation," he asserted, "render excellency, even in mean professions, an object of ambition, and frequently occasion the very greatest exertions."[29]

Emulation represented an effort to equal or surpass the work of others; it was more a striving for quality and recognition than a marketplace competition and seems to have emerged from the manner of instruction and improvement in the arts and crafts. There the striving was frequently spurred by contests and by constant measurement against the best models. The apprentice learned by copying the work of the master, but the journeyman had to go beyond copying. In order to become a master himself, he had to produce his own "masterpiece."[30]

Benjamin Franklin, having been nurtured in a craftsman's family and community, was deeply indoctrinated in the ethos of emulation and applied it in developing his philosophy of education. He believed that the best way to begin was the way his own father had begun with him; boys ought to be led "to the Shops of Artificers, and suffer'd to spend some Time there observing their manner of Working." In college, they ought to be given the history of the arts and manufactures, specifically the "History of the prodigious Force and Effect of Engines and Machines used in War." This would arouse in them "a Desire to be instructed in *Mechanicks*, and to be informed of the Principles of that Art by which weak Men perform such Wonders, Labour is sav'd, Manufactures expedited, &c., &c."[31]

Like Franklin, others undoubtedly perceived that a special mode of thinking had to be fostered to work with machines, but no one described as well as he the natural route, through art, to this understanding. "All Boys," he noted, "begin to make Figures of Animals, Ships, Machines, &c., as soon as they can use a pen." He quoted John Locke on the need for instruction in drawing, not to produce a "perfect Painter," but to acquire some "Insight into Perspective and skill in Drawing." Franklin urged going further; this was "the Time to show them Prints of Antient and modern Machines, to explain them, to let them be copied," in order to "fix the Attention on the several Parts, their Proportions, Reasons, Effects, &c." Ability to think in such a manner about machines was of value to gentlemen and to travelers, but especially to the mechanic who needed it as an essential part of his work method. With "Skill of this kind, the Workman may perfect his own Idea of the Thing to be done, before he begins to work."[32]

Not surprisingly, historians, who for the most part are not themselves practiced in this mode of thinking, have been less sensitive to Franklin's clarity on thinking about machines than to his application of emulation to another world, verbal thinking and writing. His statement in his *Autobiography* on teaching himself to write well is frequently cited, but never for what it is: a marvelously precise description of the process of emulation. He reports identifying the *Spectator* as his model of good writing, taking notes on some of the essays, and then writing out his own versions. These he compared with the original and then corrected his own attempts. Finding his word usage limited, he designed exercises to sharpen that capability and then competed against the model again. Finally he saw that he might surpass it. "I sometimes had the pleasure of fancying that, in certain particulars of small import, I had been lucky enough to improve the method or the language, and this encouraged me to think I might possibly in time come to be a tolerable English writer, of which I was extremely ambitious."[33]

Because emulation was pervasively a part of the American scene, despite the lack of guilds and the loose administration of apprenticeships, the activities of a London society based upon the principle were easily understood. The Society for the Encouragement of Arts, Manufactures, and Commerce, sometimes called the Premium Society but usually known as the Society of Arts, in fact had a specific tie to Franklin. Its founder, William Shipley, acknowledged the influence of Franklin prior to its establishment in 1754, and Franklin became one of its most honored members.[34]

Each year the Society of Arts offered a series of cash premiums to supplement the market price on specified products and offered medals for quantitative or qualitative achievements. Invention, of course, could not be encouraged as easily as output, but the society solicited the submission of inventions and sometimes awarded medals or endorsements. It focused was upon agriculture and manufactures, especially those with deep craft roots, giving only minor attention to the steam and textile machinery of the Industrial Revolution. It established also a repository of machines intended primarily for the instruction and encouragement of aspiring mechanics—again on the basis of emulation.[35] In 1772 it gave wider currency to this collection in the publication of William Bailey's *Advancement of Arts, Manufactures and Commerce, or Descriptions of the Useful Machines and Models contained in the Repository of the Society*. With fifty-five plates, it finally offered a kind of minor English theater of machines, although a trivial performance compared with the great Diderot *Encyclopédie*, with its three thousand plates, completed in the same year.

The Society of Arts projected a skewed and partial version of its interests across the Atlantic where it offered premiums for the same sort of products encouraged by parliamentary bounty: wine, dyestuffs, silk, and potash. Where needed, as in launching the potash industry, it distributed manuals of technique and offered to analyze the product. With similar motives, it sent over the model of a sawmill and gave a gold medal to Jared Eliot for his method of reducing a magnetic iron ore.[36]

Its exaggerated attention to production related to trade happened to hit just the right note during the dozen years before the War for Independence. Several colonies used the London society as a model for societies of their own, based on the principle of emulation and the offer of premiums for the production of desired goods. Boston, New York, Philadelphia, Williamsburg, and Charleston all tried this approach. Most successful was the New York Society of Arts, which operated a market and a linen factory employing three hundred and published lists of premiums on potash, linens, stockings, and shoes—not all, of course, products in harmony with the mercantile policies of the mother country.[37]

But the Americans missed direct contact with one activity of the London society that underlined a fundamental truth about technology and those who work with machines. This was its encouragement of the mechanic arts and the fine arts by exactly the same efforts to stimulate emulation. Premiums were offered for works of art just as they were for manufactures and inventions. This process resulted in art exhibitions and assemblages of paintings parallel to the society's repository of machines.[38] Art and technology had a shared genealogy running much further back than the artist-engineers of the Renaissance, but by the eighteenth century they had reached a point of divergence. It was becoming easier to forget that the same kind of nonverbal thinking remained at the center of each.

Long before the end of the War for Independence, Americans began speculating and even laying plans for the encouragement of those technologies and productions which might aid in the development of the country. Inescapably, Society of Arts methods arose as a possible approach, and John Adams even succeeded in getting the Congress to pass a resolution urging that each colony establish "a society for the improvement of agriculture, arts, manufactures, and commerce"—that is, a society of arts. Adams understood particularly well the process of emulation, defining it later as "imitation and something more—a desire not only to equal or resemble but to excel." He predicted, "Emulation next to self preservation will forever be the great spring of human action."[39]

After the war, on a rising tide of cultural nationalism, a plethora of societies and other efforts to stimulate American development arose. The general philosophical societies in Philadelphia and Boston applied effort to the improvement of agriculture and manufactures, but not very effectively. More utilitarian societies also appeared in the major cities, some with comprehensive objectives within the scope of the useful arts, others emphasizing agriculture or manufactures exclusively. The agricultural societies talked about establishing model farms but, dominated by gentlemen farmers, limited themselves primarily to the verbal methods of the philosophical societies, to the publication of written essays. The manufacturing societies, especially those in Philadelphia and New York, were a little more successful; they launched factory production of textiles, using the closest approximation they could get to the new English machinery. The New York Society first employed

Samuel Slater on his arrival in America in 1790, and it was he who, under private auspices, established the first successful Arkwright-type spinning factory at Pawtucket.[40]

The state legislatures responded, too. New York and Pennsylvania made loans to selected manufacturers who proposed to introduce different industries, and Massachusetts bought models of textile machinery and made these "state models" available to those who wished to copy them. Most significant were the patents which several states began to issue to individual inventors who proposed improvements they represented as benefits to the public. From the seventeenth century, individual colonies had occasionally granted patents, following English patent practice. Now the states from Massachusetts to Georgia began awarding numbers of patents, or conditional and time-limited monopolies, for mechanisms in manufacturing, transportation, and miscellaneous fields.[41] The standards and terms varied widely and this was one of the areas where some hoped that the Federal Convention of 1787 would be able to establish common requirements.

That convention, of course, had many priorities it judged more pressing than the encouragement of invention and mechanization. It was primarily concerned with the need to find a basis for granting the federal government sufficient revenues and powers to act effectively in external trade and foreign affairs. Despite degrees of shared nationalism, there was little disposition to grant powers not absolutely imperative, and most delegates did share a conviction that the role of the federal government should be very restricted in internal affairs.

The convention gave some consideration to writing into the Constitution a presidential cabinet, to be called the Council of State, which would include a secretary of domestic affairs with responsibility for recommending measures to forward "the state of agriculture and manufactures, the opening of roads and navigations, and the facilitating of communications."[42] This concept showed understanding of the great needs of the nation in internal development, but it never had a chance. Too few delegates had the vision of Gouverneur Morris, who predicted that the time was not far distant "when this country will abound with mechanics and manufacturers." Yet among the additional legislative powers favored by James Madison and Charles Coatesworth Pinckney were three significant provisions: (1) "To encourage by proper premiums and provisions, the advancement of useful knowledge and discoveries"; (2) "To grant patents for useful inventions"; and (3) "To establish public institutions, rewards and immunities for the promotion of agriculture, commerce, trades, and manufactures."[43]

The first and third provisions reflect directly Society of Arts philosophy; the government would encourage emulation by its own award of premiums and by even more intrusive intervention in the economy. This of course flew in the face of the congenial laissez-faire atmosphere. It would have moved the balance of state-federal power too far toward the federal government in internal affairs, and, perhaps most unacceptably, it would have cost money. By contrast, the patent power had none of these disadvantages and yet seemed to offer effective encouragement for the generally laudable objective of invention and mechanical improvement. Moreover, the example of Great Britain was visible; it had not used direct intervention, as had France, and its bounties were something less than governmental premiums. Its great success in mechanizing key aspects of its economy, notably the steam engine, the new iron technology, and textile production, seemed to rest measurably upon its patent system.

For the Constitutional Convention, the case was open and shut, but the opposition of the Society of Arts to the patent process had more meaning than usually perceived. That society refused to grant a premium for any device that had already been patented. It went further; it required recipients of its awards to agree never subsequently to accept patents for their inventions.[44] This restriction was a function of its deep-seated opposition to secrecy, and indeed the society had helped materially to breach traditional craft secrecy. On the other hand, its premiums rested entirely upon the market economy, just as did the patent system. It viewed its medals and awards as less of value in themselves than as endorsements that would help their recipients win acceptance and profit in the marketplace.

Opposition to patents had still deeper roots in the ancient

antagonism to monopoly; this had not been removed in England by the Statute of Monopolies of 1624, which laid the foundation of the English patent system.[45] That act had sought to turn the much criticized, court-granted monopolies in more widely beneficial directions. The patents that resulted were term monopolies, granted in recognition of original or imported inventions conceived to be of public utility. A patent moved, then, in opposite directions; after the expiration of a fourteen-year monopoly, an invention became freely and publicly available for all to use. This intrinsic contradiction of purpose introduced tensions that remained a part of every subsequent patent system.

Nevertheless, the convention inexorably rejected premiums and direct intervention in favor of the patent provision that emerged in the final Constitution. That succinct clause combined patents with copyrights, giving Congress the power "To promote the progress of Science and useful Arts by securing for limited Time to Authors and Inventors the exclusive Right to their respective Writings and Discoveries."[46] This was the provision most specific to the encouragement of invention and the economic activities involving mechanization.

George Washington's first message to Congress went far beyond a call for action under the patent clause. Having presided over the convention, he knew as well as anyone what had been left out of the Constitution, some delegates hoping that certain specific but unstated powers were embraced within those granted to the Congress while others hoped that the unstated powers were denied. Under his initial charge of providing "for the common defense," he asked Congress to "promote such manufactories as tend to render them independent of others." Backhandedly, he assumed that general measures for the "advancement of agriculture, commerce, and manufactures" did not need his recommendation. In asking for action on patents, he revealed clear understanding of the enormous importance to the United States of the transfer of technology, something not even hinted at in the Constitution. He urged "giving effectual encouragement as well to the introduction of new and useful inventions from abroad as to

the exertions of skill and genius in producing them at home."
Then, perhaps because he had been so active himself in canal
endeavors, he did not mention cutting canals—a power Franklin had tried unsuccessfully to have incorporated in the Constitution—but did urge congressional provision for post roads—
a proposed power also excluded. Curiously, he never alluded
to copyright, although he discussed at some length the promotion of "science and literature"—possibly within a national
university.[47]

The Patent Act of 1790 did not make provision for patenting
foreign inventions and otherwise deviated from British practice
by providing for a close examination of patent applications.
"Any useful art, manufacture, engine, machine, or device, or
any improvement therein not before known or used" was
eligible for a patent if the secretary of state, the secretary of
war, and the attorney general, or any two of them, should
"deem the invention or discovery sufficiently useful and important."[48] Specifications, drawings, and, if possible, a model,
were called for in support of each patent application. The
three cabinet members revealed the direction of their hopes by
calling themselves "Commissioners for the Promotion of Useful
Arts."[49] In practice, Thomas Jefferson, secretary of state,
became administrator of the system and presided over the first
efforts to grapple with what was patentable.

Washington retained to the end of his life the hope that
Congress would support American higher education, prefer-
ably by maintaining a national university. This would have had
the potential for forwarding technological development through
planned coursework. Benjamin Rush, for example, advocated
that the national university offer instruction in eleven "arts and
sciences," three toward the top of his list being agriculture,
manufactures, and commerce. Rush was particularly solicitous
about the promotion of manufactures, a movement in which
he had led since 1769.[50]

Washington did not need to remind Congress that even
without an explicit constitutional provision respecting agriculture, manufactures, and commerce, they had means for promoting those interests. Chief among them was the first power

under the Constitution, the laying of "Taxes, Duties, Imposts, and Excises," and the third, the regulation of "Commerce with foreign Nations."[51] The Tariff of 1789 was little more than a revenue measure, although tilted slightly toward the encouragement of manufactures. The duties established were somewhat higher on certain manufactures already being produced in the United States.

A more comprehensive program for the encouragement of manufactures was projected in Alexander Hamilton's *Report on the Subject of Manufactures*, but by that time the air had been well warmed by debate on the subject. The *Report* satisfied few and ultimately had limited effect. Manufacturers, battered by high labor costs and scarce capital, were particularly dissatisfied. Tench Coxe, the best-informed advocate of manufactures, provided the basic information and effectively collaborated in the production of the report. Both Hamilton and Coxe consciously abandoned Adam Smith's laissez-faire approach. Coxe went further, proposing protective tariffs on manufactures including outright prohibitions on some products, abolition of coastal trade duties, government construction of both canals and roads, direct federal loans to manufacturers, and land bounties. Hamilton was unready to include most of Coxe's far-ranging proposals, seeking more than he to rely upon market forces. Hamilton did urge protective tariffs and suggested serious consideration of direct government participation in manufacturing, especially of arms. He strongly supported patents, and he, too, urged that they be extended to cover the introduction of foreign inventions. He also advocated two of the primary approaches of the Society of Arts.[52]

Hamilton proposed creating a fund from the public revenues to support "pecuniary bounties" for "new and useful branches of industry" and to recognize "invention and the introduction of useful improvements." He also projected a second fund to support the "operations of a Board, to be established for promoting Arts, Agriculture, Manufactures, and Commerce." The report had little direct effect, except perhaps in the establishment of the government armories, and the Society of Arts promotional methods were disregarded totally. The government's means for stimulating improvement remained largely limited to patents and tariffs—plus a readiness to intervene more directly when a strong enough case could be made.[53]

Yet the philosophy of emulation persisted. Men saw in emulation a kind of elemental force that had an indelible relationship to technology, no matter what the fate of premium systems and societies of arts. It described the process by which the skills and dreams of millennia of artisans had been passed on to their successors. Words cannot get to its essence, although "competition" explains something of the mechanism. For the artisan, it was essentially nonverbal. He watched every motion and operation of a skilled, experienced craftsman; he looked over and felt the best models he had, copying them and then searching for undreamed conceptions—and building them. Every inventor knew what emulation was, and so did every mechanic who had to keep a machine running and every farmer who had to repair a broken plow or refashion the spindle of a spinning wheel. In such work they thought spatially, and therefore emulation came naturally to them, since it was the best approach the ages had found for cultivating the spatial thinking required in technology.

The leaders of the new United States had surprising familiarity with technology and were responsive to the opportunities it offered the new nation, but they were uncertain what policies and what degrees of intervention were advisable in encouraging development. Their extensive political experience and acquaintance with the best wisdom of the time led to their great success in setting the new nation upon a firm political foundation. A group of delegates was anxious to do as well for the transfer of the new machine technology and its application to the improvement of the country. Some of course disagreed how far this was desirable, but the limited action taken by the Constitutional Convention and the early Congresses was less a matter of disagreement than of uncertainty about how to intervene beneficially in the process. Experience was largely lacking, as was accessible wisdom from England and France. The easiest advice to follow was to do least: let each man compete to his own best advantage, and perhaps the machines and production would take care of themselves.

Probably Washington was not using the phrase out of context when in his first inaugural he invoked the aid of the "invisible hand."[54] As far as technological development was concerned, nobody else was in charge. The one positive, specific provision in the Constitution, the patent clause, turned out to be far less important than a kind a folk understanding of the ways of technology and a bubbling up of enthusiasm for mechanization.

The Steamboat

THE STEAMBOAT "came true" first in the new United States. The fullfilment of the dream of the steamboat dramatized the mode of thinking of the inventors and projectors, their antic- ipation of personal gain harmonized with social benefit, and the mechanical and business support they required. It also tested the intention of national leaders of relying primarily upon market forces and the patent system to encourage the mechanization they understood to be essential to material development.

It all came to a focus on August 26, 1791, when eight U.S. patents were issued to five applicants: for boilers, engines, and steam propulsion generally.[1] This was the long delayed resolution of conflicts that had marked a series of individual efforts to design steamboats for use on America's rivers. Remarkably, not one of the patentees had experience with steam engines, and none found adequate mechanical skills to draw upon. Yet they, and numbers of other Americans, had become excited by the prospect of something new under the sun: a boat that, regardless of wind and tide, could stem the current of America's great rivers and turn those barriers against road travel into natural highways. The prospect had been effectively demonstrated to members of the Constitutional Convention, many of whom had taken time out from their deliberations to witness John Fitch's steamboat in the summer of 1787.[2] Since then, the steamboat advocates had pushed hard for a patent law and then for the issuance of patents.

The naked idea of the steamboat was not original with any of the projectors; it had arisen almost with the steam engine itself, and mechanically propelled boats antedated even that. Thomas Savery, best known for his 1698 steam engine patent, also designed a boat driven by side paddle wheels and powered by men turning a capstan. His steam engine was scarcely an engine at all, but rather a steam pump for sucking water into an evacuated chamber and then pushing it to a still higher level by the direct force of steam.[3] The application of steam to water propulsion awaited Thomas Newcomen's piston engine, which was being developed in the same period and was available for use at least by 1712. This cranky atmospheric engine curbed the explosions that were a hazard of the Savery engine by using very low pressure steam, but although widely applied to the pumping of mines where coal was plentiful, it used too much fuel and was too bulky to be practicable on a boat. Nevertheless, the idea attracted steamboat inventors from Jonathan Hulls in 1736 to the Marquis de Jouffroy in 1783. It had limited possibilities of success. Until Watt's steam engine—which embraced a piston pushed by steam rather than by atmospheric pressure, a separate condenser, and, after a time, the double-acting principle—only a relatively ineffective steamboat was possible.

The personality contest between John Fitch and James Rumsey, the initial American contenders, has so dominated attention that important aspects of this beginning have escaped notice. Why, for example, should three of the initial steam patents have been awarded for the "improvement of Savery's steam engine"? The United States had little demonstrated need for a water-pumping engine that could conceivably be used for the propulsion of vessels only through some form of water jet. More important, why was Rumsey's patent for the relatively inefficient mode of propulsion by water or air jet, and why did Fitch abandon his ideas of paddle wheel propulsion?[4] The major contenders were curiously misdirected in failing to begin with the paddle wheel and a Watt engine.

The answers embrace the whole inventive process, but several reflect the enormous influence of one man—Benjamin Franklin. Of all the American national leaders, Franklin knew more of the ways of technology from the inside than any other. He knew more than any other American about the different modes of encouraging technology in Britain and France. He knew the manner in which the Society of Arts encouraged emulation by the award of premiums; he knew the ways of the Royal Society and their views of the relationships between science and technology; and he knew intimately leaders of the rising provincial societies in the heartland of the Industrial Revolution: the Lunar Society in Birmingham and the Manchester Literary and Philosophical Society. But most fresh in his mind when on September 14, 1785, he returned to Philadelphia from his extraordinary ministry to France were the Académie des Sciences and the scientists and inventors of Paris.[5]

With him, Franklin brought a paper he had written partly to reduce the tedium of the Atlantic crossing. Usually known as the "Maritime Observations," it has been most celebrated for his plot and description of the Gulf Stream, but it contained as well a miscellany of rambling observations, many of them reflecting his French experiences and discussions. It represented a continuing dialogue, directed to one member of the French circle, and was not at all written with respect to American needs or interests. Franklin reflected the disenchantment shared in France with the paddle wheel, agreeing that it had proved ineffective when applied to mechanical boat propulsion because of the loss in that component of force pushing up and down against the water. He, no more than his predecessors, recognized that the problem was less the efficiency attained than the deficiency in power provided by the human and animal sources that had been used.[6]

He quickly moved to the "singular" mode of propulsion suggested by Daniel Bernoulli, who proposed moving a boat forward by reaction as water was forced out its stern. Franklin added the thought that water might be pumped in from the bow and that "a fire-engine [i.e., a steam engine] might possibly in some cases be applied in this operation with advantage."[7]

Before the "Maritime Observations" was read to the American Philosophical Society and months before it was published in the society's *Transactions*, word of Franklin's criticism of paddle wheels and of his suggestion of jet propulsion began to influence steamboat development. First to be shaken up and redirected was John Fitch, that tall, ungainly wanderer from

Connecticut who only the month before Franklin's return had presented steamboat plans to the American Philosophical Society in Philadelphia and to the U.S. Congress in New York. Like almost everyone else, Fitch was ready to defer to Franklin's views on how a steamboat might best be constructed, and he spent anxious days trying to discover what those views were. He was more than ready to yield first place to Franklin in developing the steamboat, and he quickly made Franklin's endorsement his most immediate goal. Fitch was more hurt than angry when the Philadelphia patriarch declined support, and much as he revered Franklin's opinion, he had enough sense of mission to keep going.[8]

His crusade for building a steamboat began, as he told it, at a very specific time and place. He was well indoctrinated in the mythology that celebrated invention as an individual creative act occurring in an identifiable "flash of genius," a doctrine later given legal sanction by the U.S. Supreme Court.[9] John Fitch, "inventor of steamboats," as he called himself, recorded the moment of creation precisely. He was limping along a dusty road near Neshaminy, Pennsylvania, when a gentleman passed him in a horse and carriage. Immediately the thought struck him, "It would be a noble thing if I could have such a carriage without the expense of keeping a hors [sic]"; perhaps the "force procured by Steam" could be applied to the purpose. He fell into a deep pattern of thought as he tried to imagine possible mechanisms and combinations, becoming inaccessible to the queries of his companion. Hurrying back to his room, he sketched out the possibilities that had occurred to him, but, after playing around with the idea for about a week, decided that a boat might be more feasible because it would encounter less resistance on a flat body of water than a carriage moving over rutty roads and inclines. The more he thought of this the higher his enthusiasm rose until he could sense no ceiling over the realm of the possible. "What cannot you do," he mused, "if you will get yourself about it."[10]

Despite the appearance of failure that always hung about him, Fitch had already registered improbable successes in diverse fields. Most deeply an artisan or mechanic, an artist in the broad sense, his experiences were understandable within the American environment but would not have been likely in the more structured British society and even less in Continental countries. One trial turned him against seafaring and he was first apprenticed as a clockmaker, but this did not turn out well because both of his masters, Benjamin and Timothy Cheney, kept him at brasswork without teaching him clockmaking. This, however, he turned to good account by establishing a successful trade as brass founder in Windsor, Connecticut, and on the side engaging in potash manufacture and teaching himself clockmaking. When he moved to Trenton, New Jersey, in 1769, he undertook silversmithing with still greater success, employing several journeymen and attaining a net worth, according to his account, of £800. His few known silver products exhibit good design, but the war disrupted this business, and he moved, with no apparent hesitancy, into gunsmithing. With twenty men under him, he undertook the repair of arms, and surveying and land jobbing when he acquired claims to tracts of western land.[11]

In skill, Fitch never became celebrated at any of his trades, but individual skill, after all, was a recurrent casualty in the long march toward mechanization. He had more rare talents, precisely those most essential to invention; he always perceived the whole system of operation that usually comprised a number of separate skill-demanding jobs. He had the ability to get on top of each system he confronted and to think his own way through its three-dimensional problems to inventive solutions. His *Map of the North West* represents an almost improbable exercise of this virtuosity. Cartography was a fine field for the application of spatial thinking, yet most cartographers limited their efforts to placing their data on a map projection and perhaps to drawing the finished map. Fitch, in the case of this map, carried out every one of the operations involved in the whole system, of which drawing the map was only a single element. He conducted the surveys that provided new data for correcting the previous maps; he drew up the map incorporating this data; he hammered out a block of copper and polished the resulting sheet; he engraved his map upon it; he printed copies from this plate; and he marketed them himself![12]

John Fitch had resolved some extraordinarily different and

difficult problems in manipulating the nonverbal, mechanical world—but none so demanding and exhausting as the steamboat. A few weeks after his vision, he was at first shocked and then encouraged when the Reverend Nathaniel Irwin showed him descriptions and a plate of a Newcomen engine in his copy of Benjamin Martin's *Philosophia Britannica*. He sat down like the artisan-engineer he was and produced paper designs for modifying that engine so that it might be fitted into a boat. He also thought out various propulsive schemes and means of coupling the engine to them. After moving to Philadelphia, he made use of other publications with relevant information, among them James Ferguson, *Lectures on Select Subjects*.[13]

Next he required support, intellectual support from those qualified to evaluate his plans and financial support wherever that could be located. In Philadelphia, he had some acquaintances, the most important of them the Reverend John Ewing, Provost of the University of Pennsylvania, who was an investor in the land development project Fitch worked on. Ewing gave him an encouraging letter and no doubt advised him on presenting his plans to the Congress in New York and the Philosophical Society in Philadelphia. In August he prepared a brief account for the Congress, and a substantial account, comprehensive drawings, and a model for the Philosophical Society. Both the limitations and the understanding represented in his conceptions at this point are remarkable and revealing.[14]

He understood the Newcomen engine, but he had no knowledge of Franklin's concepts prior to his return, and he may have had no information about Watt's advances. He had never seen a working engine, and therefore much of his design represented his own mental combinations based on limited information and images. He planned to use a Newcomen engine with two cylinders served by two spherical boilers.* He improvised by venting the piston at the top of its stroke and by using springs to raise it after the atmospheric pressure had pushed it to its lowest point. For propulsion, he proposed either an endless belt of paddles or paddle wheels with col-

* See page 62.

lapsible floats or paddles that would fold down as they emerged from the water. Paddle wheels were the most obvious solution, and Fitch specifically remembered having seen them on a boat powered by oxen in Boston Harbor. To convert the reciprocating motion of the pistons to the rotary motion of paddle wheels, he used a ratchet, as did Read and Stevens, and Jouffroy in France; it was a readily accessible solution. Fitch ran chains from his pistons around a ratchet wheel that was rotated first clockwise and then counterclockwise by the movement of the pistons; the ratchets engaged a concentric wheel permitting it to rotate in only one direction, and thus the paddle wheels were given intermittent or interrupted motion.[15]

Especially in terms of the small relevant experience Fitch had had, he produced a commendable, imaginative design, capable of development. His second draft was simplified, incorporating the influence of "Gentlemen of Learning and Ingenuity" familiar with mechanisms. Even his primitive terminology was sharpened; tubes became cylinders, stoppers became pistons, and doors became valves. He pointed out that steam engines were already in use for pumping and that other designs might be preferable to his.[16]

Franklin's impact upon his thinking was immediate and permanent. He gave up all thought of paddle wheels and resisted the later efforts of Oliver Evans and William Thornton to bring him back to them. Except for Henry Voight's opposition, he would almost certainly have tried a version of Franklin's jet propulsion. Each of the boats he built used a form of crank and paddle propulsion, the deep genesis of which may just possibly have come from Franklin, who knew about Bernoulli's onetime suggestion of powered oars as a means of propelling boats.[17]

From Congress, Fitch asked "encouragement" in the form of its purchase of four thousand of his maps for educational purposes; this would provide the financial support necessary for Fitch to develop and build a steamboat. From the Philosophical Society, he sought answers to several questions about the feasibility of the steamboat. Congress declined to vote the support requested, and the Philosophical Society failed in Fitch's mind to raise any problems but what he "had thought of before." He felt grievously insulted by Congress' refusal of support but encouraged to seek other means of financing by the lack of negative reactions in the Philosophical Society.[18]

Again, a complex of possibilities occurred to him: the endorsement of major public figures such as Franklin and Washington might cut the knots; the state legislature might give either patents or direct support; a private stock company could mobilize the needed money; and even foreign support was not out of the question. Although full of resentment against "the Ignorant Boys of Congress," he held with intensity to the common conviction that an invention should benefit the inventor, his country, and "The World of Mankind in general." The belief that these objectives were in complete harmony was a great source of strength upon which nearly all inventors and promoters drew.[19]

Franklin having eluded his pursuit, Fitch was even more anxious to gain George Washington's endorsement as he began to approach several state legislatures for monopoly privileges. Ultimately, he succeeded in obtaining such patents from five states: Pennsylvania, New Jersey, New York, Delaware, and Virginia, and in June 1786 a committee of the Pennsylvania Assembly recommended lending him £150 to develop his boat—but the full house in a close vote declined. The letter of recommendation he hoped to obtain from Washington did not follow from the visit he made in November 1785. The most far-reaching results of Fitch's descent upon Mount Vernon were to confirm the worst rumors he had heard about a man named James Rumsey and to inform Rumsey of Fitch's steamboat projections. Washington was well acquainted with Rumsey and told Fitch that he was experimenting with a mechanical streamboat or pole boat designed to move upstream against the current, actuated by the force of the current. After some hesitation, he also conceded that Rumsey had mentioned the possibility of applying steam. He then wrote to Rumsey informing him of Fitch's activity.[20]

James Rumsey denied Fitch's claim to priority in the conception of the steamboat, dating his own speculations back to 1783 or 1784. Whenever steam did first enter his thoughts, he had been working with the mechanical propulsion of boats a year, and maybe two, before Fitch gave his attention to the question. The route by which he came to his great quest is interesting. Born in 1743 on the Maryland Eastern Shore, he came of a favored family, although his father was a struggling farmer. Rumsey was probably apprenticed as a blacksmith, but his early success was as a millwright. In 1782 he established a milling partnership in Slippery Creek, Maryland, and the next year moved across the Potomac to Bath in western Virginia, where he managed a mill, built houses, and entered an inn partnership. He undertook building for George Washington, and with his influence he was appointed, in July 1785, chief engineer of the Potomac Company for extending navigation by building canals where needed. This project was close to the general's heart, and Rumsey's inventiveness was important to him; he declared his "very favorable opinion of" Rumsey's "mechanical abilities."[21]

Rumsey's vocational mobility was not unusual, but his mechanical inventiveness was, especially in backcountry Virginia. A complete canal route would have solved the problem of moving upstream against the current, but that could not soon be accomplished and Rumsey began to contrive a mechanical boat that might move against the current, propelled by the current itself. Toward this objective, he worked with Dr. James McMechen, who as early as 1783 petitioned Congress for "premiums" in recognition of a pole boat or streamboat, and in 1784 Rumsey petitioned in his own name, McMechen agreeing in writing that the invention was Rumsey's. The design was to apply power from a water wheel mounted on the boat to move set poles against the riverbed, forcing the boat forward against the current. In May, Congress granted Rumsey thirty thousand acres of land west of the Ohio, on condition that within a year he build a boat that would run fifty miles a day for six consecutive days. Three states separately granted him exclusive rights for using the boat.[22]

This was the boat, a model of which awakened Washington's enthusiasm in September 1784 as an idea "of vast importance." Washington in turn aroused the interest of Jefferson, Madison, and Marshall in the project and became an influential factor in everything Rumsey touched thereafter. This support was instrumental in overcommitting Rumsey, bound by both the terms of the congressional grant and the canal superintendency. His first authenticated mention of steam was in November 1784 to Washington, and he did not resign his canal post until July 1786. He was never able to build a working pole boat, and it is not likely that he gave specific attention to steam until after word of Franklin's suggestions had reached him.[23]

Fitch's course of development is unusually well recorded because of his disposition to set down in words and drawings an introspective account of all his tribulations and periodically to chastise his contemporaries in print. By contrast, Rumsey has been tagged as "secretive," but he was much more typical of the artisan and mechanic, David Rittenhouse once asserting, "much writing ill suits a Mechanic."[24] Most mechanics lacked an extended verbal education; their craft heritage encouraged secrecy; and their work was primarily a series of exercises in spatial thinking, not talking.

The chronology of Rumsey's steamboat plan is largely lost. He began with exactly the same view of the Newcomen engine Fitch used, finding it, however, in J. T. Desaguliers, *A Course of Experimental Philosophy*. By the time of his pamphlet of 1788, he asserted that he had advanced to a single-acting engine with a condenser—characteristics introduced by Watt, of course. His initial boiler was an iron pot, the lid held on by rivets and solder, from which he proceeded to a tube boiler; with both he had trouble when the solder melted and pressure was lost. His iron castings were made at the Antietam Forge and later boilers by Frederickstown coppersmiths and blacksmiths; brass cocks and pistons came from Baltimore. He seems to have financed his efforts from his own and family resources, but by the time of his first public trials, December 3 and 11, 1787, he had run out of money. Rumsey sought state steamboat patents as had Fitch, but with less success. Because he failed to bring his pole boat to the effectiveness required, he lost the thirty-thousand-acre land grant offered by Congress. His steamboat moved as fast as four miles an hour, but his machinery was not reliable and further development became imperative. The boat, once tied up, never moved under steam again.[25]

Fitch reached the same point, a little earlier, in the famous trial before the Constitutional Convention on August 22, 1787, but by a route that is more instructive because more clearly marked. He was ill equipped to carry through all of the needs in building a boat but least disadvantaged in conceptual planning and development. Funding was his worst initial problem, especially when Congress, the state governments, private, and foreign patronage failed to provide the sums needed. Leaders in fields of mechanical or intellectual endeavor offered little more than mild approval, coupled with the constant refrain voiced most emphatically by Andrew Ellicott that the proposal had to be carried to a trial. To get to that end, Fitch next formed a company, with good results that surprised him; each member contributed $20, and in April 1786 he quickly raised $300. This, however, was soon exhausted, and Fitch entered on a series of struggles with the company over raising more money and over planning. The company was reorganized twice, once in February 1787 and again in 1789. Initially, Fitch held twenty of forty shares issued and voted accordingly in meetings, but successive reorganizations reduced his role to nominal equality with the other members of the company. Fitch estimated in 1791 that he had raised a total of over $20,000 from his companies.[26]

Membership in the companies changed frequently. Fitch listed nineteen continuing members, two who contributed significantly, and six who withdrew with refunds. Most were small merchants and businessmen; two, at least, he had known before bringing his vision to Philadelphia: Thomas Hutchins, the geographer, and Joseph Budd, a hatter. Richard Wells, a prosperous merchant and onetime operator of a leadworks, was a particular reliance, and Richard Stockton, a leading merchant and political figure, led the company briefly. Two members were recent immigrants, important for a time in the city's cultural life: Samuel Vaughan, who soon returned to England, and Dr. William Thornton, who after 1789 became the major stockholder and major influence in the company.[27]

Thornton had a wholly different background from Fitch's and a different spectrum of capabilities, vocations, and avocations. Born in the Virgin Islands but educated in England and Scotland to an M.D. degree, he was a competent painter and composer, a student of language, and a self-taught architect who designed the Library Company of Philadelphia building and several buildings in Washington, including the initial plan of the Capitol. Like Fitch, he speculated in land and had an unquenchable fascination with machines, which he expressed in many years of service as commissioner of the Patent Office. Thorton rescued Fitch's company at a couple of points, designed a condenser that did not help, and a boiler that did by providing a volume of steam previously unattained that brought the boat to its best speed. Thornton himself believed that his absence in the Virgin Islands from 1790 to 1792 permitted ill-equipped members of the company to insist on unreasonable changes and delays that brought the great effort to an end. His capacity for spatial thinking in a variety of fields, most notably in mechanics, was more similar to Fitch's than that of any other stockholder.[28]

After funding, Fitch's worst problem was to find the mechanics and facilities required to build his machinery. No men familiar with the new Watt engines were to be found, but three Britishers familiar with Newcomen engines were called to Fitch's attention: Josiah Hornblower, Christopher Colles, and John Nancarrow. Hornblower, member of the premier English engine-building family, had come to America with the 1753 Belleville engine and settled here, and Colles had built the New York City engine before the Revolution. John Nancarrow had built engines in England but at the time was operating a Philadelphia iron foundry with Timothy Matlack. None of the three was helpful; they seemed incapable of advancing beyond the Newcomen engine as they had known it.[29]

At a total loss for men to execute his plans, Fitch happened upon one he may not have much overpraised when he called him "the first Mechanical genius that I ever met with." Henry Voight was another immigrant, recently arrived from Germany where he had worked in a mint and had probably gone through a clock- or watchmaking apprenticeship. He spoke—and even wrote—in a heavy German accent. He was a fine mechanic, responsible for carrying the early steamboat plans to the point of functioning mechanisms and specifically for inventing several boilers and a horseboat that, with Fitch's concurrence, he patented. He and Fitch often got on well, but at one point of disenchantment Voight claimed the steamboat credit for himself, charging Fitch with being a poor mechanic. Fitch no doubt understood that there was truth in both charges; he recognized that Voight, in addition to his general capability in spatial thinking, possessed a skill and fingertip knowledge he himself lacked. As he put it, "the principal part of the original thoughts of any part of the Works proceeded from me but I could hardly propose anything but he would make some improvement upon it. And after a Plan was once adopted [I] left the Execution of it to him."[30]

Philadelphia was better equipped with shops and craftsmen than the backcountry where Rumsey worked, but the skills needed for executing the best of steamboat plans did not exist in America. Clockmakers were the finest mechanics available, but the tolerances they achieved were less than those required in working parts of a steam engine. Besides, they did not work with the same kind of materials, and the blacksmiths and brass founders who did had little experience with anything but gross tolerances. According to Thornton, "not having a single engineer in our company or pay, we made engineers of common blacksmiths."[31]

Satisfactory precision was never attained. Fitch's first trial steam engine with a cylinder of one-inch diameter was too tight to work at all, and the three-inch engine that did work varied from round by the conventional measure of the thickness of a worn shilling, far too much for a good fit. Fitting and packing, particularly of the moving piston and piston rod, was not satisfactorily solved. Yet Fitch moved from his original conceptions to twelve- and eighteen-inch engines that worked well enough to move his boats—the first one going at four miles an hour in 1787 and the second in 1790 at a maximum of eight miles an hour on a commercial schedule for over two thousand miles. Following Watt's practice, these engines incorporated condensers and double action; that is, the steam was admitted on one side of the piston to push it one way and then on the other to push it back again. Still, the noise and vibration of the engine, plus that of the linkage and propulsive machinery, was not only annoying but wearing to the machinery and the boat. Breakdowns were frequent, a consequence of unresolved design and machining problems.[32]

Fitch's propulsion illustrates the constraints within which he planned as well as the way his mind worked. Rejecting paddle wheels because of Franklin, a helical screw because it did not work well on a manually operated trial, and jet propulsion because of Voight, he came to "Cranks and Paddles for rowing" one night while he tossed in bed unable to sleep. Fitch was certainly running over in his mind all possible options, and a suggestion of powered oars may have triggered his thoughts.[33] The version Fitch first developed, with banks of paddles that raised and dipped alternately, so much resembled the paddling of an Indian war canoe that it probably reflected his experience when a captive of the Indians. He never gave up the view that some crank and paddle system was the best mode of propulsion and on the second boat merely moved the paddles to the stern.

Between Fitch's 1787 boat and the completion of the second, James Rumsey came to Philadelphia, and although he left rather quickly his impact was great. He had emerged from the 1787–88 winter realizing that he had to improve upon and rebuild his machinery and that he could do so only with more support than he could ever find in the neighborhood of Shepherdstown, Virginia. Rumsey decided to try Philadelphia, which offered the best possibility, arriving there in March with more assets than have been perceived. He brought of course the endorsement of George Washington, which was the more valuable because so unusual, but he also brought enough of his own strength to make Washington's support believable. His name, to begin with, was well known to leading Philadelphians, especially to members of the American Philosophical Society. His cousin, William Rumsey, had been a major landholder in the Bohemia region of the Maryland Eastern Shore where Rumsey himself was born, and had been elected to the society and included on the society's prewar committee to plan a Chesapeake-Delaware canal route. Also, James Rumsey demonstrated that he was not a one-dimensional inventor by including several other inventions in his newly printed pamphlet. He described an improvement in Dr. Barker's mill, a form of outward flow water turbine; a Savery-type pumping engine improvement; sawmill improvements; and a water tube boiler for use with the steam engine. Further, his mode of propelling his steamboat was inescapably the same as that proposed by Franklin.[34]

The trail from Franklin's jet idea to Rumsey has not been preserved. The "Maritime Observations" paper was finally read to the Philosophical Society on December 2, 1785, and early in 1786 Arthur Donaldson sought support from the Pennsylvania legislature for a boat to be propelled, admittedly, on Franklin's plan. Donaldson worked out his steamboat plans with the advice of Levi Hollingsworth, and Hollingsworth was particularly helpful to Rumsey after his arrival in Philadelphia. There is no clear evidence that Rumsey developed any steamboat plan until after Donaldson, and none of the affidavits on Rumsey's steam engine components antedate Franklin's return. The probability is that Rumsey consciously applied Franklin's propulsion suggestion.[35]

In doing so, he introduced a genuine invention of his own; he mounted the steam engine above the water pump and coupled the two by using a common piston rod.* But Rumsey's later designs suggest that he never solved the problems this form of linkage involves.[36]

The American Philosophical Society welcomed Rumsey as a congenial mind at their meeting of April 5 and later elected him to membership—as they never did with Fitch. They invited him to present his papers at their next meeting, but at that time encountered a curious coincidence: at the same meeting Henry Voight and a third inventor presented boiler plans identical to that of Rumsey. This was a single, twisted water tube that made several 180-degree turns within the fire chamber. The society was unable to untangle the conflict and commended all the proposals while the larger dispute moved beyond their hall. Fitch responded to Rumsey's pamphlet with one of his own, *The Original Steamboat Supported*, which was answered for Rumsey in turn by Joseph Barnes.[37]

Meanwhile, Rumsey received all the help he needed in forming a company to develop the steamboat and his other

* See page 69.

inventions. Named the Rumseian Society, the company looked like a committee of the Philosophical Society, fifteen of its twenty-one members being members of the Philosophical Society (compared with only five among the twenty-seven members of Fitch's companies). First named in every Rumseian Society list was Benjamin Franklin, who had declined all Fitch's importunities to join in his effort. Other members included William Bingham, Philadelphia's leading merchant, Samuel Magaw, a secretary of the Philosophical Society; and Levi Hollingsworth, who had known William Rumsey on the canal committee.[38]

Rumseian Society members were well acquainted with Fitch's difficulties, both financial and mechanical, and planned a route over that sea of troubles. The society first made an effort to avoid competition and to pool resources by combining the Fitch company and the Rumseian Society on an equal basis, an offer Fitch rejected with disdain. Back in 1786, Fitch had given thought to the importation of a Boulton and Watt engine but was unable to carry through that plan, which would have eliminated at least half his mechanical problems. The Rumseian Society's approach was to avoid import problems and the inadequacy of American skills and shop capacities by subscribing $1,000 to send Rumsey to England where he could buy an engine, hire skilled mechanics, and raise more money as needed.[39]

A remarkable network was pressed into action. Benjamin Franklin had not revealed his own feelings when Crèvecoeur inquired about Fitch, responding woodenly that David Rittenhouse's good opinion gave him "more favourable sentiments." But among the key letters of introduction he gave Rumsey was a letter to Benjamin Vaughan in London counseling against Fitch, "who is endeavoring to deprive him of such advantages by pretending a prior right of invention." Vaughan was a brother of John Vaughan, Philadelphia member of the Rumseian Society, active member of the Philosophical Society, and son of Samuel Vaughan who had belonged to Fitch's first company; Benjamin Vaughan accepted the role as Rumsey's unofficial advisor in England. Benjamin Rush wrote Dr. John Coakley Lettsom, a great friend of the Americans, warning against Fitch's "licentious" character, an opinion probably not fully counterbalanced by Thornton's following remonstrance in favor of Fitch. Thomas Jefferson in Paris had never even replied to Fitch's previous request for aid in obtaining a French patent, but when Vaughan asked him to help Rumsey, the American minister acted with alacrity. Jefferson entertained Rumsey when he visited Paris, introducing him to several potentially helpful people, and became a strong supporter. Miers Fisher subscribed to the Rumseian Society in the name of Robert Barclay of the London banking house. The American establishment was behind Rumsey and showed its power in opening one door after another.[40]

The most important of these doors led to Matthew Boulton's office in Birmingham, where Rumsey was received with such enthusiasm that he had reason to feel his quest had been won. Boulton was so impressed that he laid plans for a steamboat-building partnership with Rumsey and instructed his lawyer to withdraw a caveat against steamboat patents—in favor of Rumsey. With the firm's mechanical and financial capabilities in addition to Boulton and Watt engines, technical success would have been virtually assured. What Boulton offered was the production and financial help he had given Watt, neither of which Fitch had ever been able to find. Later replacement of Rumsey's relatively inefficient jet propulsion scheme by another mode would have been an easily arranged detail; Rumsey would have emerged at the center of the development and dissemination of practicable steamboats and in charge of the sale of Boulton and Watt engines in America.[41]

He refused! It takes more than a minute to comprehend how this eager mechanic, only a few months from the backwoods of the United States, could have declined so incredible a guarantee of success. Rumsey regarded as "dishonorable" the price of the partnership that required that he free himself from the Rumseian Society. Boulton did not see as feasible a partnership with the entire Philadelphia company and he saw nothing dishonorable in buying out the members, a transaction he could have funded handily. Benjamin Vaughan, hearing of Rumsey's difficulties, urged taking English workmen to Ireland and building a steamboat there where Watt patents did not obtain. Boulton, in turn, branded this advice "rascally" and turned off the whole deal.[42]

The most striking aspect of this lost opportunity was the remarkably high evaluation Boulton put upon Rumsey and his plans. He was a successful businessman who was working closely with the most celebrated mechanic in the world, and he was ready to bring an unknown American into a partnership. Boulton's acknowledged esteem for Franklin could never have carried him that far; he was captured by Rumsey's mechanical imagination and by the fine, spare design of his machines. Thus, Washington had seen more in Rumsey than a man who wanted very much to do something the general regarded as important; Franklin more than an inventor carrying out one of his schemes; and Jefferson was not wholly naive in calling him "the most original and the greatest mechanical genius I have ever seen."[43] Boulton confirmed these judgments; Rumsey was an unusually imaginative inventor.

In fact, Boulton never dropped him entirely; he withdrew his opposition to Rumsey's patenting a boiler and wished him well in his endeavors. Rumsey went on to obtain three English patents and to build a steamboat with English workmen and largely with English capital. He found out, however, that English mechanics, too, were ill equipped for this unfamiliar work. Before he was able to bring his boat, *The Columbian Maid*, to a satisfactory trial, he died from a stroke he suffered following a minor triumph at the Society of Arts. He had just explained to the committee of mechanics the principles of his new device for the equalization of waterwheels and had been asked to write out the form of endorsement he would like from the society.[44]

The fatal stroke occurred in December 1792, little more than a year after his U.S. patent had been granted and long enough for the law and the patent he received under it to have embittered and affected him seriously. Steamboats and steamboat enthusiasts had been strong in seeking a constitutional patent provision; they became an irrepressible voice when it came to writing the law; and steamboats were the biggest single problem confronting the first commissioners in executing the law. When the words of the law reached Rumsey in England, he reacted despondently, concluding that if it meant what it said a patent would have no value. He complained, "The Law of Congress respecting patent rights almost amounts to an Exclusion of my ever returning to my own Country," for even while he was talking to Boulton, his intention had always been to center his activities in the United States.[45] After the patents were issued, he was sure that their value was slight because the steamboat grant to him was directly overlapped by the grant to Fitch, and his two other patents were similarly overlapped by grants to other patentees. This vast disappointment, added to Rumsey's probable understanding that his boat was not going to run very well anyway, were, at the least, conditions preceding his stroke.

The Patent Commission had been at a loss to know how to resolve the conflicting claims—especially those between Rumsey and Fitch. Jefferson's strong sense of justice surely placed him in an agonizing position as chairman of the commission because he had already praised Rumsey extravagantly and snubbed Fitch. A logical resolution, especially to a politician's mind, was to arbitrate the differences between the two major antagonists. This effort, however, broke down, and the ensuing patents damaged the American patent system at its inception.[46] Patents were intended as a major encouragement of invention and technological advance, but a case can be made for the responsibility of these particular patents in bringing the feverish experimentation in steam navigation to an extended hiatus. An effective patent granted to one claimant might have gained him enough support to move effectively, but Fitch, like Rumsey, went inexorably downhill after this.

He worked in a desultory manner on a new, larger boat, intended for the Mississippi, but nothing went right and company funding dried up. In July 1792 he deposited in the Library Company of Philadelphia his valedictory and chronicle of defeat in the form of an autobiography and steamboat history—aimed at Jefferson more than any other individual. He failed to use constructively the support made available for producing an effective horseboat by John Nicholson. In 1793 his steamboat company sent him to revolutionary France to build steamboats there, a plan that backfired when the importation of the required English machinery proved impossible. Fitch thereafter went from bad to worse, bouncing from England to Massachusetts to Bardstown, Kentucky. Unlike Rumsey, his life was not taken from him, so in 1798 he took it himself.[47]

The initial pioneers failed to bring the steamboat into use. They explored all the technical concepts required for successful operation on American rivers; they correctly identified the function steamboats could perform within prevailing economic patterns. They brought the elements of the steamboat and designs of the whole system to working effectiveness—and yet their most fundamental failure was technical. They did not bring the steamboat to a point of such technical effectiveness that it could operate on accessible revenues. Their overall conceptions—"inventions"—were adequate, they mobilized large sums of money, and they made use of the best mechanics available in America and in England. They and generations after them believed that they failed because society had not sufficiently protected them with patents or sufficiently supported them with funding; and they were right to the extent that larger funding combined with effective protection might have led to continuing steamboat operation. But the deficiency of their own efforts lay in engineering effectiveness; no boat produced was sufficiently well engineered, that is, sufficiently well designed and machined, to function reliably and to meet the costs of its operation.

For a few years, steamboat enthusiasm sputtered along, depending on occasional short-distance runners, the most inventive of whom was Samuel Morey of Connecticut, who took out several patents. Morey produced a functioning steamboat, but unable to bring it into use turned aside and later produced an internal-combustion, turpentine engine that pointed toward a wholly different technology.[48] The best long-distance runner turned out to be John Stevens, Jr., one of the 1791 patentees, whose interest had been kindled only a few years earlier by the Fitch-Rumsey contest.

Stevens was a well-to-do gentleman with varied business interests and a spreading fascination with mechanical things— but no capability of his own for the work required. He was most conspicuous for his large conceptions and most hobbled by his weakness in detailed development engineering. His frequent failures and sometimes bumbling performances obscure his fundamental understanding of the nature of technology; he possessed an effective capacity for spatial thinking, and he was able to form in his own mind complexes made up of varying elements. His understanding was nowhere better expressed than in his education of his son Robert Livingston Stevens, who grew to possess not only his father's large-ranging visions but a precision, tenacity, and constructive imagination his father lacked. He planned the early training of Robert in mathematics and the elements of mechanics and, as soon as his fingers could hold them, put tools in his hands as well as paper and pencil.[49]

Before John Stevens moved beyond paper steamboat plans, he seems to have communicated his infection to his brother-in-law, Robert R. Livingston, usually known as "The Chancellor." Stevens was politically and commercially influential in New Jersey and had a very pleasant estate at Hoboken, but Livingston was significantly more powerful and influential in New York and boasted a still more imposing estate at Clermont on the Hudson. Stevens had patented a multitubular boiler that was a significant improvement over the Rumsey-Voight twisted-tube boiler—although it may very well have originated with Nathan Read of Connecticut, as the latter asserted.[50] Over many years, Stevens experimented and conducted trials on his own premises with workmen he hired and supervised. Livingston, a promoter of agricultural reform and textile manufacturing, developed steamboat conceptions of his own and tended to contract with others to build his engines and boats. As had Fitch and Rumsey, Livingston sought validation of his conceptions by laying them before the American Philosophical Society. His 1799 submission of a new steam engine and boiler he had designed revealed a process of change then under way that was moving the steamboat dream from the Fitch-Rumsey frustrations of 1787–91 to the Fulton success of 1807.

The Philosophical Society committee that received Livingston's papers turned them over to a relatively new member who had arrived in Philadelphia from England in 1798, Benjamin

Henry Latrobe. Latrobe went over Livingston's figures, which purported to show that a Watt engine lost 75 percent of its power in overcoming internal friction and resistances, and he countered the estimates of loss in each component with his own figures, which produced an almost reversed evaluation. He branded Livingston's analysis "much ado about nothing" and saw in him, as did many of his contemporaries, a visionary with little mechanical ability or sense of reality.[51]

Latrobe was a personification of the newly professional approaches to technology. His English education was not at all usual, having been raised in an English Moravian community, studied for a time in Germany, worked under the engineer John Smeaton, and finished an extensive preparation in architecture. He was remarkably trained and attuned to the material world, both man-made and natural. He was the best-qualified architect and the best-qualified engineer in America. At this moment he had just begun the execution of his plan for a Philadelphia water supply system based upon two steam pumping engines; he instantly became Philadelphia's resident expert on steam power.[52]

In this capacity he was called upon in 1803 to write another, related report in answer to the question, "Whether any, and what improvements have been made in the construction of Steam-Boats in America?" This gave him the opportunity to assess the history of the steamboat, which he believed to have led nowhere. For a while, he reported, "A sort of mania began to prevail, which indeed has not entirely subsided, for impelling boats by steam engine," and this produced modes of construction and operation different from any tried in Europe. But he concluded, "Not one of them appears to have sufficient merit to render it worthy of description and imitation." His failure to see a future for steamboats is the more remarkable in view of his immersion in the very changes that made that future certain.[53]

He was one of the more conspicuous members of a network of mechanics, engineers, inventors, and entrepreneurs engaged in raising the capability for making steam engines and indeed for working effectively with mechanisms generally. Latrobe had strengthened the most important single center of this activity—the Soho Works of Nicholas Roosevelt at Belleville, New Jersey. There the steam engines for his Philadelphia waterworks were built, produced in Roosevelt's dramatization of the transit of technology to America.

All those working with the new machine technologies depended on immigrant mechanics who often moved from one projector to another. John Hall, for example, was an English mechanic who worked for Thomas Paine on his iron bridge, on John Fitch's steamboat, and then for John Stevens. Stevens also employed Marc Isambard Brunel, who worked previously for some of the New York projectors and afterward returned to Europe to become one of England's great engineers. Even Oliver Evans, when he ventured into a new business in opening the Mars Works, depended much upon Charles Taylor, an English "steam engineer" who became his foreman.[54]

Roosevelt had begun by buying the old Schuyler copper mine and hiring Josiah Hornblower to put the original Newcomen engine back in operation. He added machine shops and employed a remarkable group of immigrant mechanics, whose training of others and progression elsewhere have been chronicled by Carroll Pursell. James Smallman brought English engine-building experience, later worked directly for Latrobe, established his own engineworks in Philadelphia, and after that in Washington. He trained Charles Stoudinger, a German, who became a reliance of Robert Fulton and in turn trained other important machinists including George and Lewis Rhode, sons of Roosevelt's German assayer, Frederick Rhode. The Rhodes themselves trained other engine builders including James P. Allaire, who became a major New Jersey manufacturer. John Hewitt had been trained in the Boulton and Watt engineworks; his son, Abram Hewitt, became a New York and New Jersey ironmaker, participant in the second iron revolution, and onetime mayor of New York City. The network became even more intricate when Roosevelt married Latrobe's daughter and both Latrobe and Roosevelt joined Fulton's Mississippi steamboat building and operating enterprise.[55]

Machine shops, foundries, and other centers of machine production often employed at least one English mechanic, men who sometimes felt they were valued only for their skills and that when these had been assimilated their value would be gone. Mechanics with good fingertip knowledge of machines, as had the English who tended less to move from task to task, possessed a stock of images that were fundamentally important in devising new mechanical systems. Yet, as Fitch had discovered, Englishmen, with an exaggerated attachment to the technological forms they knew, were sometimes too rigid to invent new forms. In fact, those closest to the skills of the operative mechanic, whether English or American, did not often emerge as leaders in steamboat development. Thornton and Latrobe were immigrants, but of a different sort. Neither brought mechanical skills but rather a rarer capacity to think in terms of entire working systems or compositions—whether landscape paintings and buildings or water supply systems and steamboats.

Oliver Evans, and to a lesser extent Henry Voight, were mechanics who enjoyed also a large vision and ability to devise new machines. Evans was most distinguished by his ability to think through wholly new systems synthetically, but he also had an analytic capability and frequently sought help from scientists at home in the related analytic disciplines.[56] Latrobe in his 1803 Report had dismissed Evans's engine, developed by 1801, as chimerical and absurd, but he was even more wrong on Evans than on steamboats. Evans's engine was already grinding plaster of paris commercially, and he continued to improve it. Evans produced the first true alternative to the Watt engine, a high-pressure engine that required no condenser, was cheaper, more compact, and best suited for many uses. The idea of using high-pressure steam was old but not practicable in the days of Savery and Leupold because of the strength of boilers and precision of machining required. Evans's engine came to dominate steamboating on the Mississippi and Ohio. As the Columbian engine, it was applied to manufacturing. It clearly preceded Richard Trevithick's version in Britain and may have provided the model. It identified the most creative of the American steam inventors and justified Oliver Evans's reaction against "the mighty and *infallible* opinions of Englishmen." As for steamboats, he was soon able to say "they have run, are running, and will run; so has my engine and all of its principles succeeded."[57]

Thus a very important change occurred; Evans, Roosevelt, Allaire, Smallman, Robert McQueen, and the West Point Foundry soon made available machining and machine-building capabilities totally lacking in the 1780s. In this heartening environment. Robert R. Livingston simply turned over his designs for an engine and boat, with a partnership agreement, for Roosevelt to build. He told the New York legislature that he had applied "a mode of steam engine to a boat on new and advantageous principles" and needed them to withdraw the monopoly previously granted to Fitch. They responded in 1798 with the requested twenty-year monopoly—on condition that he get a boat running satisfactorily within a year. Roosevelt finished the engine and mounted it in the boat in good time, but Livingston's design was unworkable; it depended upon a small, geared-up stern wheel intended to run at high speed. Tinkering did not help, and Livingston rejected Roosevelt's sound advice in favor of side paddle wheels. Instead, he went to a stern crank and paddle scheme urged by John Stevens—and the boat fell apart.[58]

Stevens made slow progress in his independent efforts. He tried a number of models, engines, and propulsive schemes; he investigated the purchase of a Boulton and Watt engine but, anxious to develop American capabilities instead, declined to pursue it. His earliest conspicuous success was the *Little Juliana* of 1804. This was a small boat using high-pressure steam, a multitubular boiler, and twin-screw propellers. Speeds of five to eight miles an hour were reported in the initial trials, and in 1844, with restored machinery and a new boat, she made eight miles an hour in American Institute tests. Her engine and boiler are preserved in the Smithsonian Institution.[59]

Stevens and Livingston kept in touch, sometimes on a friendly basis and sometimes in a posture of conflict. In 1801, however, Livingston went to France as American minister—taking with him his steamboat dreams. There he met Robert Fulton, and the foundation for final success was laid.

Robert Fulton is best viewed as an artist-artisan who became

an engineer and an entrepreneur; his background had similarities with those of Fitch and Rumsey, but he had fine arts
dimensions more similar to those of Thornton and Latrobe.
Beginning as a miniaturist, he left Philadelphia for London in
1787 to study painting and was received graciously by Benjamin
West, as many of his fellow Americans had been before him.
Although overwhelmed by the skill and accomplishment he
found in the art world, he worked assiduously for at least four
years to improve himself. He painted, corrected, repainted,
and reworked his canvases—in the manner West always insisted
upon—but by 1791 began a drift into new endeavors and by
1793 had pretty much abandoned painting. His painting skill
did not flower as he had hoped.[60]

He admired Benjamin West extravagantly, envying most the
great recognition he enjoyed and his status in society; parallel
achievement in some field continued to be his goal. Fulton
turned to the design of a variety of mechanical systems: to
canal engineering, to the steamboat, and to undersea warfare.
In these endeavors, his capacity in drawing and painting, while
inadequate to bring him distinction in the art world, proved an
important reliance. Drawing ability helped first in thinking out
his conceptions, then in presenting them, and finally in preparing his own excellent illustrations, as in his 1796 *Treatise on
Canal Navigation*. Throughout, the beckoning inducement of
West's fame continued. Even after his spectacular success in
introducing the steamboat he wrote the painter, "I am endeavoring to be in the mechanical arts what you are in the fine
art of painting."[61]

From the Society of Arts in 1792, he won a silver medal—
for the invention of a marble-cutting machine. He may have
met James Rumsey at the society or even as early as 1786, when
both men were in Bath, Virginia, for intervals. In any case,
they came to know each other in London, and Rumsey inescapably communicated some of his steamboat enthusiasm to
the younger man.[62]

Fulton also became acquainted with several other men of
large vision in technology, including the Duke of Bridgewater,
the prime figure in English canal building, the Earl of Stanhope,
steamboat projector, and Edmund Cartwright, inventor of the

power loom and of a ropemaking machine. Fulton gave extensive attention to canals, approaching them as a total system for which he applied technological solutions in each problem area. He obtained a 1794 patent for raising canal boats by ramps, and he projected canal-digging devices, aqueduct plans, and methods for devising canal networks. He was unable to sell canal plans in either England or France or to profit from his tanning process or flax-spinning machine.[63]

While he was developing his engineering capability and style in these efforts and beginning to call himself a "Civil Engineer," he increasingly pursued the steamboat, especially after he moved to Paris in 1793. There Joel Barlow, who had also befriended Rumsey, proved his most important supporter both in steamboat and in undersea warfare projects. In fact, Fulton lived for many years with Joel and Ruth Barlow. He tested his steamboat ideas on small models that quickly led him to abandon a fishtail propulsive plan and confirmed him in the view that hull form was critically important. Then, early in 1802, Fulton met Livingston, recently arrived from America.[64]

The two men quickly came to a meeting of the minds and executed a contract calling for Livingston to put up £500 and Fulton to build a trial boat in England. If successful, Fulton would design and supervise the building of a boat to ply the Hudson between New York and Albany, the two men sharing equally in the profits. Fulton had already carried out studies and experiments related to the steamboat that he financed largely from his underwater warfare commissions, most of which came from England. For the New York project, Livingston's financial support seemed sufficient.[65]

His next needs were adequate engineering design and adequate mechanical skills. In working out his design, Fulton followed a significantly different path from those of earlier projectors. His only purpose was to produce a boat that would run satisfactorily, not to produce a new invention and not to obtain a patent for the purpose of recognition. In fact, he did not even seek a patent until long after his boats had succeeded. He read and experimented and he collected all the data available on previous steamboats; from William Thornton in the Patent Office he obtained copies of all the steamboat patents. In his own hand, he copied sections from Fitch's autobiography, wherever he may have obtained it. Thornton believed, although Fulton denied it, that he got plans of Fitch's French boat project from Aaron Vail. From Livingston he heard details of Livingston's own efforts, plus those of Stevens and Morey. From Rumsey he got information on his plans. Somehow, he seems to have obtained information on the *Charlotte Dundas*, a steam sidewheel tugboat built by William Symington in Scotland in 1803. He was well informed about the French trials of Desblanc and Jouffroy.[66]

Most of Fulton's experimenting was in terms of the whole boat, although he did study boiler design and propulsive systems. His approach to the engine is particularly instructive. He never gave any thought to building an engine himself but regarded it as a black-box component to be purchased on the basis of specifications he would give the builder. Another index to his approach was his use of Mark Beaufoy's *Nautical Experiments*, which provided quantitative data on the resistance of differently shaped solids to motion through water. From this data, added to his own, he hoped to be able to calculate in advance the speed and characteristics of a boat and, by the same process, to design the best proportions of length, beam, and draft.[67]

His first boat was built not in England but in France. Completed in 1803, it had side paddle wheels, a borrowed steam engine, and features Fulton had been working on for more years than either Fitch or Rumsey had spent in active steamboating. Before a trial could be held, however, Fulton had to endure a harrowing experience he was never able to forget. During a storm the engine tore loose from its moorings, fell through the bottom, and the boat ignominiously sank. When repaired, it made only three miles an hour, not fast enough to be useful, and Fulton had to content himself with the belief that he now had enough data to improve the next boat.[68]

In fact, conditions were already being laid for the success of his New York boat. Livingston had importuned the friendly legislature a third time, and the new grant required only that the two partners run a twenty-ton boat at the rate of four miles an hour to secure a twenty-year monopoly on all New York waters. On his part, Fulton ordered a steam engine made to his specifications by Boulton and Watt. True, he had to use all the influence he could mobilize to obtain the required license for exporting the engine, but, that, too, came through in sufficient time. Regarding Boulton and Watt as the experts, Fulton also asked their best advice on what sort of boiler to use, how to arrange the components, and the effect of using salt water in the system. His final move to assure technical success was to engage at least one mechanic who had worked for Boulton and Watt to cross the Atlantic and set up the engine.[69]

The *Steamboat*, or *North River Steamboat*, later called the *Clermont*, made no more than five miles an hour on her run to Albany and back, but that was enough to launch the world into a new era, not alone of steamboating but of powered transportation generally. A big boat, 133 feet long, it conformed to Fulton's ideas of proportion and form with its narrow beam and flat bottom and sides. There was nothing new about the twin sidewheels or the methods of linkage. Its most important characteristic was success; it was a success of engineering design.[70]

Fulton did not immediately seek a patent because he did not need one; the New York monopoly was not overtly based upon a claim of invention and therefore much preferable to a patent, which might have required an impossible defense of priority, utility, and novelty in steamboating. Besides, Fulton was as aware of his predecessors' disastrous experiences with patents as he was of their technical plans. Yet competitors arose who challenged the monopoly in the courts, alleging that Fulton had invented nothing; in their attacks they built up Fitch as the true inventor, making him into a heroic figure unjustly defeated by society. By 1809 Fulton became convinced that some sort of patent was necessary but even then was ready to claim none of the components, only the proper proportions that he asserted to be critical to success. His enemy, Thornton, was still in charge of the Patent Office and beat Fulton to the punch by issuing to himself a patent for contributions he said he had made to the Fitch boats. Still, he issued Fulton the patent requested but continued to complain that proportions were not patentable and that, anyway, Fulton's proportions were exactly the same as Fitch's.[71]

It did not matter; his boat was a creative engineering design, unique to its designer in the same manner that a painting is a unique creation. Indeed, Fulton's method had something in common with that of the painter who paints over elements that fail to relate satisfactorily to other parts of the picture. His boat was a composition that differed from other boats as a Stuart portrait of Washington differs from other portraits. In all his work, he kept meticulous records of how the alteration of one component relative to others had changed performance. In the finished steamboat, he felt a justifiable pride of creation that did not pertain so much to the moving vessel as to the understanding, ideas, and design behind it.

Fulton believed in "mental property," yet that concept and even the broader ideal of the patent obscures the creativity involved in every mechanical construction and often in adaptation and repair as well. Fulton's steamboat did not deserve a patent, but patentability is not to be directly correlated with creativity. His work was creative, even though not one of its components was original, as was the work of every predecessor who got a boat running. To establish the deserved credit for contributions possessing originality, priority, and utility in so complex a mechanism as a steamboat would require a massive computer analysis of generations of effort based upon data that does not exist. The very ideal of the patent grievously distorts the technological process, and the case of the steamboat illustrates this effect with clarity.[72]

Fulton's rapid success in developing steamboating on New York waters under the protection of the monopoly led him to plans for similar steamboat empires on other river systems, especially the Mississippi, where he, like Fitch and Stevens, anticipated the steamboat's greatest day. John Stevens, barred from New York waters by the monopoly, sent his *Phoenix* through the open sea in 1809 to inaugurate continuing steamboat service on the Delaware. Fulton tried and failed to get control of steamboat development on the Chesapeake and failed elsewhere except on the lower Mississippi. Nowhere else was he able to obtain matching monopolies and once he had demonstrated the practicability of steamboats, men arose quickly to build their own and to improve upon his. His *New Orleans* was the first boat on the Mississippi in 1811, but it did not become the model for later development; its ship's hull was slowly succeeded by forms more like his first steamboat. Under the pressure of competition, a gradual evolution of the western boats occurred, with Henry M. Shreve and Daniel French among the innovators. On the wide, shallow waters, a low-draft, square-hulled boat emerged, and the engine was raised a deck higher. The boats were built cheaply, indeed shabbily—except for the ornate saloons and public rooms; on the still shallower Missouri, the stern-wheeler came to predominate.[73]

The most significant deviation from the original Fulton model was the engine. Within ten years, the high-pressure engine pioneered by Oliver Evans dominated the entire river system. It was smaller, cheaper, and less complex; its large fuel consumption was not a serious problem so long as wood remained plentiful. However, the hazards feared before anyone ventured to build high-pressure engines were dramatized in America with boiler explosions that frequently extracted a toll of life. Foreign visitors felt that Americans accepted the accidents easily, but in fact the outcry led to federal regulation in 1838.[74]

The steamboat was indeed something new under the sun, and its first realization in the United States was not a result of public policy. The patent system, upon which the founding fathers had much depended for the development of new technology, had positive effects only in the anticipation; in practice, its effect upon steamboat development was detrimental until after Fulton's success. Specific efforts to promote the steamboat by the most important national leaders, primarily in their support of James Rumsey, had negative effects. Even immigrant mechanics, whose migration was encouraged, did not play leadership roles; their major responsibility was raising the American capability for the machine practice required to build steam engines and boats.

The successful breakthrough of 1807 rested upon two factors: the good engineering of Robert Fulton and the economic opportunity made effective by the New York State monopoly applied to a route not served by competitive alternatives. The economic opportunity depended upon a widely perceived need for improved internal transportation that could be most readily achieved on the great rivers by a satisfactory powered boat. This particular economic pull was not strong in either Britain or France, where alternative transportation fulfilled needs better. In addition, primarily because the United States was less developed materially and economically than the two European countries, but also because of its set of mind against regulation and control, economic restrictions were less weighty here.

Some of the American advantages were countered by disadvantages; Britain and France had better access to capital, to some of the mechanical skills required, to certain entrepreneurial experience, and to scientific advice. And both Britain and France contributed to the success in America. The manner in which Fitch, Rumsey, and Fulton wove back and forth among the three countries is significant, to say nothing of the transatlantic lives of Thornton and Latrobe, or Voight, Taylor, Smallman, Hall, and the other immigrant mechanics. The steamboat illustrates well the North Atlantic character of much emerging technology.

The advantages and disadvantages America offered in developing the steamboat were integrated into the thinking of each of the promoters. Their activity rose and fell as the fate of patents, legislative monopolies, financial support, and social attitudes fluctuated. Nevertheless, the mind of the individual inventor or projector was the ultimate key. That mind could be turned on or off and its direction altered by external factors, but its quality and mode of thinking were beyond the reach of proximate forces. The men who emerged as most effective in developing designs of complete steamboats based upon individual and unique combinations of a complex of elements all enjoyed a capacity for spatial thinking. Among them, Fulton, Fitch, Thornton, and Latrobe had previously shown creative spatial thinking in quite different fields—in art, architecture, crafts, or cartography.

National leaders had been anxious to develop policies and laws that would encourage technological development, and in the patent system they sought specifically to encourage the contriving mind. However, Benjamin Franklin's insight into how that mind worked was not matched in others, although the wide acceptance of the process of emulation embraced at least external understanding of mental processes. Even Franklin failed in applying his insights to the steamboat. Government policies did not work as intended, but neither inventors nor foreigners could miss the strength of motivation and the still rising intention of Americans to encourage invention and innovation. The steamboat was hailed in America, as Fulton and his predecessors had known it would be. In turn it became a model to encourage future projectors of other machines. More notable than the fumbling manner in which America struggled toward realization of the steamboat was the still rising enthusiasm for mechanization wherever it might conceivably work.

- 3 -

Steamboat Images:
A Pictorial Essay

THE STEAMBOAT projectors and inventors arrived at their conceptions by manipulating and rearranging images in their minds. They necessarily began with images familiar to them, some drawn from adjacent fields of experience and some from unrelated fields, from book illustrations, or from their visualization of words they heard or read. The new components they devised usually derived from preceding, familiar forms. All of their steamboat designs possessed uniqueness and originality, even when they sought only to duplicate what they understood to have been accomplished by predecessors.

The steamboat, as the nineteenth century came to know it, had a few indelible characteristics: its engine, its paddle wheels, and its boilers that too often exploded. The steam engine gave the boat its name, but the paddle wheels came to seem almost equally a part of its definition. The American builders had to combine concepts that were initially very vague: partial images of engines and propulsive devices, including paddle wheels, with linkages and boilers they might have known in other applications and could modify.

The mental images of the steamboat builder have to be the historian's most important quest. He can never reach them directly, but illustrations known to have been used are basic sources, original drawings come very close to mental conceptions, and machinery components embody the concepts.

Figure 1. Desaguliers 1744 view of a Newcomen engine

THE NEWCOMEN ATMOSPHERIC ENGINE

All thoughts of steam propulsion were premature prior to the development of the Newcomen engine. Thereafter, many made plans for such an application and a few conducted trials, the Americans depending upon book illustrations for their initial understanding of the mechanism. Here the two principal projectors began with exactly the same image of the Newcomen engine, Rumsey finding it in the Desaguliers plate and Fitch in the Martin plate of just a few years later. Fitch asserted that he had never heard of a steam engine, let alone seen one, and there is no reason to imagine that Rumsey had seen one either.

This use of the same Newcomen engine view by two men who were not in communication with one another is less coincidental and surprising than it appears. It had been copied and reengraved for the Martin plate, just as it had been from an earlier source for the Desaguliers plate. This view appeared first in 1717 and continued to be used to illustrate the Newcomen engine into the nineteenth century. Rather than "a" view of the engine, it became "the" view.

Once the concept of the atmospheric engine was communicated to mechanics familiar with air or even with water piston pumps, the mechanism became immediately understandable. It was simply a pump run backward: the differential in gas pressures being converted into mechanical work rather than the reverse. Neither the pictured mechanism, however, nor the 1753 Belleville engine could be applied directly to the propulsion of boats. These enormous, ungainly stationary engines were not suitable for installation on a small boat.

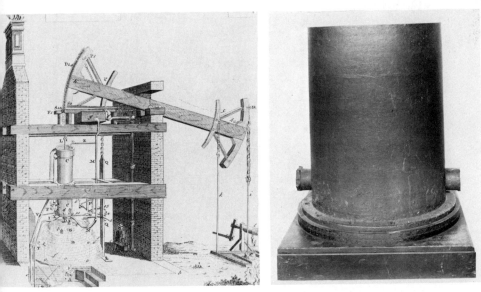

Figure 2.
Martin 1747 Newcomen engine

Figure 3.
1753 Belleville, N. J., Newcomen cylinder

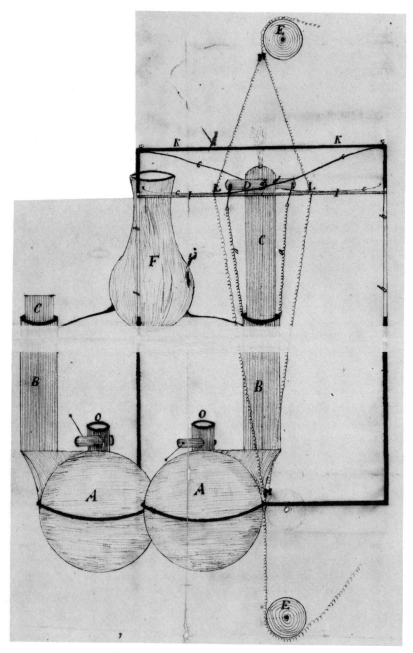

Figure 4. Fitch Newcomen engine, 1785

Figure 5. Symington Newcomen engine, patented 1787

NEWCOMEN ENGINES ON STEAMBOATS

John Fitch was innocent of any knowledge of James Watt's advances, specifically even of single-acting steampower and the condenser, when he designed his first engine for steam propulsion. Like Hulls and Jouffroy before him, he thought out an atmospheric engine that might work on a boat. In plans he submitted to the American Philosophical Society on August 1, 1785, he pictured two vertical cylinders served by a common reservoir above them that would cool the cylinders and condense the steam by spraying water into them. Instead of a weight, which might swing or bind on a boat, he used springs to raise the pistons. To convert reciprocating motion to circular motion, he used a ratchet wheel rotated by ropes running over pulleys from the piston rod frame.

The triangularity of William Symington's Newcomen engine intended for boat propulsion is externally striking in its similarity to Fitch's. So is his use of two cylinders and ratchet drive.

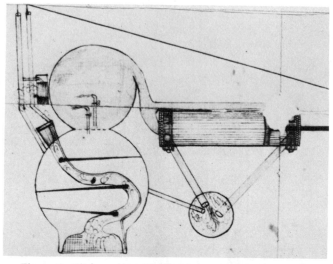

Figure 6. Fitch engine with Watt improvements, circa 1787

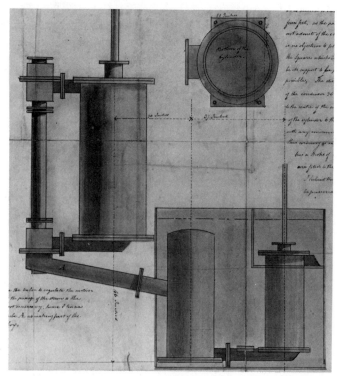

Figure 7. Fulton Boulton and Watt engine, ordered 1803

Figure 8. Evans high-pressure engine of 1811

IMPROVED STEAM ENGINES

Fitch used a single-acting, condensing engine in his first boat and a double-acting engine by 1789. Information about these advances of Watt reached him relatively early in his efforts, and he easily assimilated the concepts into engine design. This sketch clearly shows steam being admitted alternately to each end of the cylinder and being drawn off into a condenser from each end. He may have drawn it long before he built his first boat. There was a long development period between such a conceptual sketch and a working steamboat based upon it.

Fulton's 1803 engine drawing accompanied his order for the engine that, when finally delivered and installed, powered his 1807 *Steam Boat*. He consulted with Boulton and Watt about modifications he felt were needed for his intended use in a steamboat—which intention he did not reveal.

Evans built a successful high-pressure engine as early as 1803 and designed and redesigned several subsequently. His Columbian engine of 1811 was particularly successful and widely used.

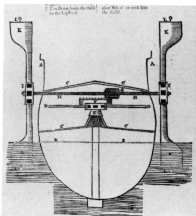

Figure 9.
Vitruvius paddle wheel, 1511

Figure 10.
Savery paddle wheel, 1704

PADDLE WHEELS

The antiquity of paddle wheels is presented in the 1511 picturization of Vitruvius's first century B.C. description. This shows a single wheel turned by a manually operated crank. More current in the English-speaking world was John Harris's *Lexicon Technicum* of 1704, which presented Thomas Savery's design for manually operated paddle wheels in which several men turned a capstan located on a covered deck. It was generally understood that paddle wheels had never succeeded very well—even when powered by horses or oxen.

During his ministry to France, Benjamin Franklin became acquainted with the attitudes behind numerous efforts to improve the paddle wheel. The Académie des Sciences approved one 1710 invention of self-adjusting paddles that held them nearly vertical as the wheel rotated. This answered the same criticism to which Franklin responded in his "Maritime Observations": that there was too much loss from the upward and downward component of the force exerted by rotating paddles. His illustration exaggerated this effect by immersing the wheel to its axle.

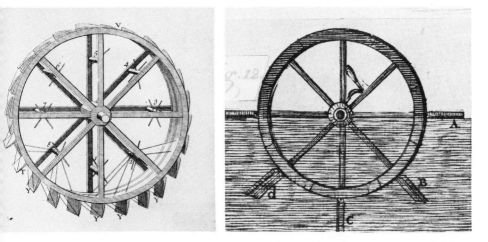

Figure 11.
Wheel with self-adjusting paddles, 1710

Figure 12.
Franklin paddle wheel, 1786

Somehow, John Fitch had become aware of the paddle wheel criticisms even before Franklin's return. His initial proposal was for paddle wheels with self-adjusting paddles—or an endless chain of paddles. Either design would have reduced the loss from upward and downward force components.

Figure 13. *Fitch endless chain of paddles, 1785*

Figure 14.
(a) Franklin jet boat, 1786

Figure 14.
(b) Bernoulli jet boat, 1753

JET PROPULSION

In France, Franklin also learned of Daniel Bernoulli's propulsion proposal that had won the académie's 1753 prize. This called for pumping a jet of water out the stern to drive the vessel forward by reaction. Not published until 1769, although Bernoulli had initially hinted at the idea in 1738, it was still fresh during Franklin's mission. Franklin had enjoyed debating such questions with his French friends, and he enjoyed suggesting a minor modification in his paper—that the water be pumped in from the bow, presumably facilitating its flow out the stern.

He had neither the intention nor the expectation that this contribution to a French dialogue would provoke the reaction it did in America. On the authority of Franklin, Rumsey was more than ready to design and build his steamboat on the principle of jet propulsion, and he found that this association was a great advantage in winning support. Fitch's mind was already prepared by his knowledge of paddle wheel criticism to view jet propulsion favorably. He sketched different designs for such a boat and, somewhat against his will, was talked out of building one.

Figure 15. Rumsey jet boat, 1788

Rumsey's boats must both be considered failures. Under the governing conditions of available engines, boilers, and components, the jet boat was inferior in comparison with available alternatives.

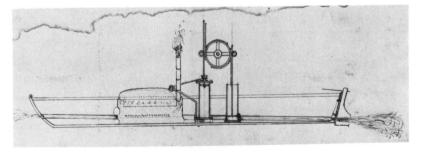

Figure 16. Fitch jet boat, circa 1786

Figure 17. Fitch 1787 crank and paddle boat

CRANKS AND PADDLES

John Fitch's crank and paddle plan was an imaginative response to the criticisms of paddle wheel effectiveness. It was a continuation and development of the thinking that had led him to propose the use of self-adjusting paddles or an endless chain of paddles. Fitch's mechanism lost very little of the force applied in downard and upward motion because each paddle entered and left the water in a nearly vertical position. This design certainly represented an evolutionary development from his first ideas.

At the same time, the resemblance of the boat to an Indian war canoe, with its banks of paddles moving in unison, is more than coincidental. Fitch had directly observed hostile Indians in canoes, notably just prior to his capture during the War for Independence. He had a realistic view of Indians, guarded and defensive but respectful. He never gave up his opinion that some form of crank and paddle design offered the best means

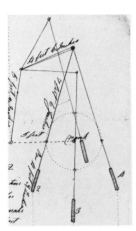

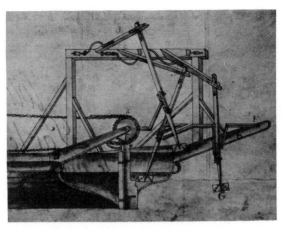

Figure 18.
Fitch stern paddle plan

Figure 19.
Fitch 1790 stern crank and paddle boat

of propelling steamboats. His 1787 design, then, was put together from different sorts of images: some drawn from previous efforts to design propulsive systems and some from the observation of Indians paddling a canoe.

This boat made no more than five miles an hour and was plagued with frequent breakdowns. In his 1790 boat Fitch moved the paddles to the stern, and this is certainly the boat pictured in his U.S. patent application, which was granted in 1791. This shows three paddles, each separately activated by its own crank. His French patent of 1793 pictures exactly the same boat, redrawn.

The speed of eight miles an hour attained by this boat was not exceeded by any steamboat until well after Fulton's 1807 success. This was the boat that ran over two thousand miles on a commercial schedule between Philadelphia and Burlington. How much the improvement it represented depended upon overall design, including the cranks and paddles, and how much upon boilers, condensers, and machining, cannot be estimated.

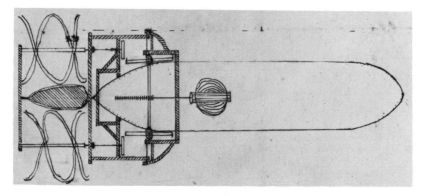

Figure 20. Fitch "screw of paddles," circa 1786

PROPELLERS

Fitch's "screw of paddles" represented still another modification of the paddle in his mind. His drawing clearly pictures twin helical propellers designed to be used underwater. It is not surprising that his manual trial of propellers on a small boat did not show promise. It is surprising that he immediately thought of using two propellers, the form in which John Stevens successfully applied the propeller in his *Little Juliana* of 1804. Perhaps the influence of matching side paddle wheels or side cranks and paddles was responsible.

Figure 21. Stevens propeller, 1804

Figure 22.
Thornton paddle wheel, 1809

Figure 23.
Fulton paddle wheels, 1809

BACK TO PADDLE WHEELS

Although neither Fitch nor Rumsey ever turned to paddle wheels, their experimentation with alternative propulsive designs eliminated those approaches for their successors. Later projectors were less inhibited by the authority of Benjamin Franklin, and most of them came to regard steam propulsion in terms of paddle wheels. Several drew up plans and a few tested them, the most successful being Samuel Morey, who ran the first of two paddle wheel boats in 1794.

By 1807, Fulton encountered little encouragement to try any other means of propulsion, although he weighed several; his success on the Hudson established paddle wheels as the form his successors would use. Thornton, knowing well the characteristics of Fulton's 1807 boat, decided in 1809 that Fitch's patent was void and granted himself a steamboat patent incorporating a stern paddle wheel. This stimulated Fulton to take out his patent based upon the side paddle wheels his boats were already using.

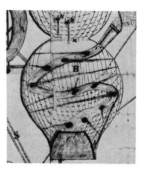

Figure 24.
Savery boiler

Figure 25.
Fitch boiler, 1785

Figure 26. Fitch
fire tube boiler, 1786

BOILER DESIGNS

It was early understood that a sphere was the ideal vessel to withstand steam pressure. Just such a spherical boiler was made known in published views of the Savery engine, and Fitch initially sketched out a similar boiler. This, however, he soon modified by placing within it a spiral fire tube to conduct the hot gases through the water in the sphere. The source of the spiral tubing is less clear, but it was commonly used in distilleries. In practice, the spherical boiler was not feasible because it could not be manufactured satisfactorily.

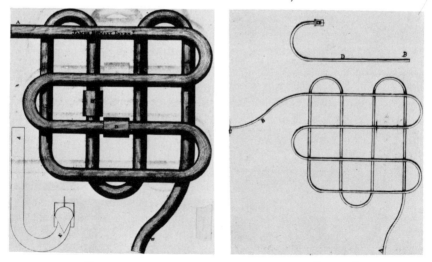

Figure 27.
Rumsey water tube boiler, 1788

Figure 28.
Voight water tube boiler, 1788

Figure 29. Stevens porcupine boiler, 1804

Among the great diversity of boiler drawings left by the steamboat projectors, the most dramatic may be the single water tube, which made several 180-degree turns within the fire chamber. Both James Rumsey and Henry Voight submitted designs for this that were identical except in the diameters of the tubes.

John Stevens and Nathan Read both claimed to have originated the multitubular boiler. A variety of this was the porcupine boiler, but it was not initially practicable because of inadequate materials and machining capabilities.

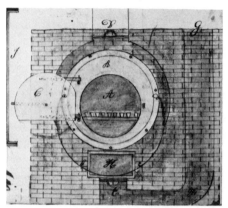

Figure 30.
Fitch locomotive model boiler,
circa 1798

Figure 31.
Evans "Cornish" boiler,
circa 1803

PRACTICABLE BOILERS

Many ingenious boiler designs had to be shelved, not because the abstract designs were unsatisfactory, but because they were not suited to current manufacturing capabilities. Beside them, simpler forms of the boiler emerged out of long experience. In many industries, boiling meant building a fire beneath an open vat, but such processes as distilling required closed systems. There, a firebox was usually placed beneath the boiler and the hot gases conducted under the boiler bottom to its opposite end where they were led up a flue. This design lent itself easily to the use of a cylindrical boiler that could be produced from rolled copper or wrought iron and that had the advantage, for containing steam under pressure, of a circular cross-section.

At least as early as 1796, Oliver Evans began making cylindrical boilers with the firebox placed inside an inner cylinder, or truncated cone, running the full length of the outer cylinder. Thus, the firebox and extended flue for conducting the hot gases to the rear of the boiler were encased within a water and steam jacket. His drawing of about 1803 brought the hot gases back under the bottom to a vertical flue near the front. This boiler, usually called the "Cornish" boiler, became very widely

Figure 32. Fulton boiler, 1809

used after 1812 when Richard Trevethick demonstrated it in Britain.

How much it was known in the United States before then has never been clear, but a curious steam locomotive model survives, probably made by John Fitch during his final days at Bardstown, Kentucky. Hauntingly, this has a firebox cylinder within a cylindrical boiler.

Fulton's patent drawings of 1809 show a more conventional boiler of the type used by Watt. Indeed, this may well represent the boiler of the 1807 steamboat, which was a rolled copper boiler manufactured in England. The firebox is located under the patent drawing boiler, and the hot gases were undoubtedly led to the rear under the boiler bottom and back to the front flue along the sides—as Watt often did.

Figure 33. Fitch Map of the North West, 1785

Figure 34. Fitch creamer, circa 1775

OTHER REALMS OF SPATIAL THINKING

Several of the steamboat projectors, conspicuously Fitch, Thornton, Latrobe, and Fulton, achieved notable success in other fields of spatial thinking. Perhaps the most dramatic of these was mapmaking, preeminently a spatial field that requires the translation of three-dimensional spatial perceptions to a two-dimensional medium—a process similar to that so fundamental in machine technology. Fitch's achievement in carrying through all the operations in producing his Map of the North West was certainly a prodigy. Latrobe had a much more extended career in mapmaking, both for canal and for geological survey maps. Thornton entered mapmaking through land speculating—as had Fitch.

Fitch worked in several of the arts and crafts, contributing at the highest aesthetic level in silversmithing, this creamer representing satisfactory contemporary design. Latrobe and Thornton were more outstanding and more diversified in their attainments, both reaching their peaks in architecture.

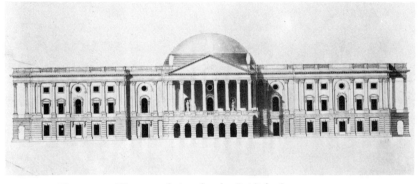

Figure 35. Thornton design for the Capitol, circa 1795–97

ENGINEERING AND THE ARTS

Architecture necessarily has both art and engineering dimensions. Because architects must always be concerned with both the engineering and the aesthetic aspects of their buildings, it was not unusual for architects to carry out engineering and technological roles unconnected with architecture. Both Thornton and Latrobe demonstrated this relationship of capabilities. Latrobe was better trained and more successful in architecture, but both men played roles in planning the national

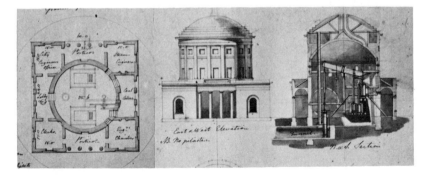

Figure 36. Latrobe design for the Center Square Engine House, 1799

Figure 37. Fulton design for a canal aqueduct, 1796

Capitol and intersected at other points. Latrobe was better trained in engineering, too, but his careers with the navy and in planning municipal waterworks were somewhat paralleled by Thornton's in the Patent Office. Latrobe's classical building in which he squeezed the Center Square pumping engine symbolically united his worlds of art and architecture with steam and engineering.

Fulton had no architectural career, but his art career, successful primarily in portraiture, was linked to his engineering through the spatial thinking required in each. His art also influenced his engineering designs directly, giving his drawings an architectural quality. Among the drawings he made and engraved for his *Canal* book, he gave priority to the canal aqueduct, which he presented almost as a piece of architecture in a traditional landscape. His facility in drawing gave his views of machinery a clarity and three-dimensionality that at least suggest a clarity of thinking behind them.

Figure 38. Fulton self-portrait, circa 1807

FULTON'S ART AND STEAMBOATS

Fulton aspired earnestly and strove diligently in painting, an art ostensibly unrelated to engineering and steamboats. Art critics have dismissed his canvases as unimportant, but art remained important to him and therefore important in understanding him. This portrait is presumed to have been painted shortly after his 1807 success, and it is superior to some of his early work, which shows questionable competence. The fine eye for detail required in portrait painting was just as essential in mechanical technology; the sense of overall spatial design that was critical in catching the appearance of an individual was the essence of good machine design.

Before Fulton applied for his first patent in 1809, he had turned over machine drawing to others, but they worked very closely under his supervision and produced excellent renditions of machinery. This view of the *Steam Boat* was probably an accurate view of the rebuilt boat that had made the 1807 trip to Albany, by now already being called the *Clermont.*

Figure 39. Fulton 1809 patent drawing of the Clermont

- 4 -

The Telegraph

THE ELECTROMAGNETIC telegraph, like the steamboat, was something new under the sun. It was not an improvement within an existing technology, and it was not a combination of existing capabilities put together in answer to a clear social need. It appeared when it did because not until then had it been possible. The door was opened by the new knowledge of electricity developed by Ampère and Oersted and of electromagnetism by Sturgeon and Henry. This understanding was the precondition for the telegraph, and consequently it has been labeled the first science-based invention, although scientists were outnumbered by others who sought to rush through the door opened by the new knowledge. Indeed, in the United States and throughout the non-British world, an artist became identified with the invention of the telegraph, Samuel Finley Breese Morse.

Morse's system of telegraphy was the first to succeed in America where it rapidly overcame competing systems, and it spread to much of the rest of the world. Yet Morse was neither a scientist nor a mechanic; he might be described as the most prominent American artist of his day. A talented painter with accomplishments and potential well beyond those of Robert Fulton, he was president of the National Academy of Design and professor of the literature of the arts of design at New York University—the first professor of art in the country. How could a recognized art professor turn away from art and succeed in using new scientific capabilities to create a genuinely new technology?

The accomplishment took place in a nation greatly changed

during the fifty-odd years since Fitch and Rumsey had found little help from scientists, inadequate mechanical capabilities, and an unprepared economic and social community. By 1840, when Morse took out his first patent, the United States had for some time enjoyed "sustained economic growth" incorporating rapid technological change. Boasting a population of 17 million spread over thirty states, the United States was already one of the three leading industrial nations in the world with a growing per capita output that approached that of Great Britain.[1] More to the point of Morse's quest, the business community had a new order of capability in mobilizing capital, in putting together combinations, and in accounting. The rapidly emerging scientific community had a strong sense of its importance and destiny, but at the same time its new professionalism sometimes inhibited its aid to technology. Machine tools and modes of technological production, including the "American System of Manufacturing," had made striking advances, although in the new field of electricity there was not yet much market production.

As for the Industrial Revolution, the Americans had transferred what they wanted of it and had probably drawn equal to Britain in textile invention and innovation. The steam engine was an integral part not only of internal transportation but of much American manufacturing, especially in the newer branches. Even Britain's coal-based technology had finally penetrated and iron reduction by anthracite as well as by coke was coming in. The government now was less hobbled by parsimony, except during the depth of the Panic of 1837, but its leaders were still not agreed on whether or how to aid technology and less driven by noble dreams than the founding fathers.

The particular telegraph Morse brought to this scene was more clearly one man's brainchild than the steamboat, which had so many parents, although many men were also involved in Morse's telegraph. Still, Morse was so central in this development that much of the inventive process can be perceived by examining the quality of his imagery and thinking and the narrative of his personal struggle to bring the telegraph to fruition.

To begin with, Morse had a favored background, although

not one that ostensibly encouraged either art or technology. His father, the Reverend Jedediah Morse, was one of the intellectual leaders of the Congregational church. Yet he had also achieved creative success in a distinctly visual or spatial field—geography. His pioneering American geographies so captured the school market that his son was nicknamed "Geography" Morse. Moreover, when Finley, as he was known in the family, manifested an early talent for art, his father supplied him with drawing paper and then with a camera obscura. Both parents were warm, supportive of Finley and his two younger brothers, and flexible in their own expectations. From this home, all the boys emerged with religious conviction, patriotic dedication, and a strong sense of rectitude; Finley was especially marked by an irrepressible drive to succeed.[2]

At Yale College, he developed in unexpected directions. In contrast to his brothers who followed him there, Finley was never a good student, especially not in Latin or literature, graduating a year late in 1810. He did enjoy his science courses: chemistry with Benjamin Silliman, in which he made models of the batteries demonstrated; electricity with Jeremiah Day; and formal assistance in electrical experiments under Sereno Dwight. Even more he enjoyed hunting, brandy, cigars, and dancing, with the unavoidable result of continuing indebtedness. He also made extracurricular excursions into art, painting a mural in his room depicting *Freshmen Climbing the Hill of Science* and undertaking a series of miniatures for college friends and townspeople, spurred by the opportunity to apply the proceeds to the reduction of his debts.[3]

Morse left college knowing the road he wanted to travel; he was, he reported, "made for a painter." The reading of Silliman's journal had given him a longing to "travel with improvement" to himself "and to society," and acquaintance with Washington Allston convinced him that painting could be the route to success and the good life. Allston, a rising American artist resident in London, was here on a visit, and the two men responded well to each other. Morse's parents demurred for a time, convincing him to try employment with a bookseller in their hometown of Charlestown, Massachusetts. The young man was orally articulate and later proved an effective polemical writer, but the culture of words and of books was never congenial to him.[4]

As he fretted, he painted: a watercolor of his family, an oil of *The Landing of the Pilgrims at Plymouth*, and a couple of others. They were enough to convince Allston, Gilbert Stuart, and his parents that his talent might be developed.[5] When Allston sailed for England, Morse accompanied him, funded by his father. In London, all he had hoped for seemed confirmed, especially when he came under the tutelage of Benjamin West, who appeared to Morse, as he had to Fulton, the ideal model of American success in art.

William Dunlap repeated a delightful story, illustrative of West's methods but more deeply symbolic of the ways of art itself—and of the practice of emulation. When Morse showed him his drawing of the Farnese Hercules, West responded, "Very well, sir, very well; go and finish it." Morse unhappily answered that it was finished, but West replied, "Oh no, look here, and here, and here." Twice again, with the same results, Morse returned with his drawing, finally declaring, "I cannot finish it." West then delivered his moral, "Now sir, you have learned more by this drawing than you would have accomplished in double the time by a dozen half-finished beginnings. It is not numerous drawings but the *character of one*, which makes a thorough draftsman."[6]

Following in the footsteps of Rumsey and Fulton before him, Morse soon found his way to the Society of Arts where he submitted a terra-cotta sculpture of *The Dying Hercules,* a study preparatory to an oil painting. Even West was pleased when it won a gold medal, exclaiming, "I have always told you any painter can make a sculptor."[7] Both the finished canvas, which won praise but no prize at the Royal Academy, and the ensuing *Judgment of Jupiter* were large historical paintings in the genre most approved for the exercise of the greatest art by West and Allston. Although Morse worked with sculpture, portraits, and landscapes, he felt that these did not call forth a "grandeur" of thought. Significantly, historical paintings were not interpretations of existing three-dimensional scenes. They required the free mental manipulation of component images until the composition took on the imagined feeling. The range of possible designs was wide and the models were the greatest; for Morse they included Titian, Raphael, and Michelangelo.[8]

This expanding dream came to an abrupt end when, after four years, Jedediah wrote that he could no longer support his son's studies. Morse returned home to engage in what by then had come to seem an improbable quest. "If he meets with encouragement," Allston wrote, "he will be a great painter," but that was the question.[9] In America, no earlier artist had made a successful career of historical painting, the only pursuit Morse saw as acceptable. He believed that this was not merely a personal goal but one that his country must make possible for its own fulfillment.

With all his vigor and imagination, both of which he possessed in large measure, Morse launched a heroic effort, but the exhibition of his *Dying Hercules* in Boston and in his rented studio in Charlestown did not awaken the support he needed.[10] The direct approach failing, he undertook, as a temporary reliance for subsistence, what turned out to be a long career in portraiture. In Boston, Concord, the Connecticut Valley, and Charleston, South Carolina, he found good markets for his portraits, and as he progressed his effectiveness as a portraitist improved. By 1822, ready for another direct assault on his objective, he spent months in Washington painting portrait studies of eighty congressmen for inclusion in a patriotic canvas of the *Old House Chamber in the Capitol*. A fine example of painting in the grand manner, it required all his talents in thinking and redesigning, painting and rearranging to obtain the desired effect. Yet neither in Boston nor in New York did it attract enough paid admissions to cover its costs.[11] Another enormous effort failed.

Through several years after his return from Europe, Morse remained uncertain whether or not he was gaining on his goal. Once he thought of studying for the ministry but decided against it. Then he did carry through some serious efforts in a wholly different field—mechanical invention. Wealth from patenting an invention had become an appealing dream to many. For a time, for example, a rash of truss bridge patents was granted to inventors who recognized the financial rewards that might come to the man who designed a cheaper way to make railroad bridges. Morse and his brother Sidney experimented briefly with steamboat designs and then turned to a new pump, intended primarily for use in hand-operated fire engines. He had little success in selling this "flexible-piston pump," or less seriously "Morse's Patent Metallic Double-Headed Ocean Drinker and Deluge Spouter," although he tried to peddle it on some of his portrait-painting excursions. Sidney finally reported that it was the same thing as a pump published by Benjamin Martin fifty years earlier.[12] Morse himself decided that "an inventor earns his money hard," but nevertheless went on to invent a marble-cutting machine with Hezekiah Augur, a New Haven grocer and carver turned sculptor. This in turn proved unpatentable because too similar to Thomas Blanchard's famous stocking lathe.[13]

Inventing remained a possible route to wealth and acclaim, but, sticking with art for the moment, Morse in 1825 transferred his base to New York City, by then the great metropolis and the center of the largest American art community. He moved at a good time professionally, just after having executed the city council's commission for painting the official portrait of Lafayette during his formal visit to the land of his second citizenship. The relocation, however, almost coincided with the sudden death of his first wife, Lucretia, a tragedy even his New York successes could not fully overcome. He moved easily into the circle of William Cullen Bryant, James Fenimore Cooper, and Richard Henry Dana, and he quickly became the leader of a vigorous group of young, practicing artists. Having thought of establishing an art academy in New Haven and having succeeded in some measure in Charleston, he contemplated taking over leadership of the moribund American Academy of the Fine Arts from the aging president and fellow émigré from Connecticut, John Trumbull.[14]

Instead, he combined with the active artists to form, first, a drawing society and then a competing academy, which they named the National Academy of Design, with Morse as president. They used the word "National" because any other would have suggested inferiority to the American Academy, although when a joint committee explored union of the two academies, it proposed a more accurate name, the New York Academy of the Fine Arts.[15] The effort broke down, however, and the National Academy continued, indeed still survives, while the American Academy faded away.

The word "Design" in the title was even more significant. According to Morse, this was not merely a semantic matter; the arts of design embraced "painting, sculpture, architecture, and engraving while the fine arts [included in addition] poetry, music, landscape gardening, and the histrionic arts." The arts of design, then, involved the spatial composition of multiple elements while the remaining fine arts, which Morse excluded, were sequential, chronological, or verbal. Predictably, the academy used premiums to encourage "industry and emulation," and, lest anyone mistake the meaning of emulation, Morse advised students "to imitate the model before you precisely . . . you must consider your models *perfect* while you are learners." Echoing the dual concern of the London Society of Arts with both fine and useful arts, he insisted that "Painting and its sister arts of design" belonged "in the train of the *useful* arts," in fact were "their *avant couriers.*"[16]

Morse began to flourish. He made efforts to develop relationships between the National Academy and art communities in other cities, corresponding especially with John Neagle in Philadelphia and Henry Pratt in Boston.[17] He became active in the New York Athenaeum and was asked to deliver its annual series of lectures for 1826 in the Chapel of Columbia College. These he worked upon assiduously, conscious that they were the first course of lectures on art ever given in the country, and he was rewarded with general approbation. Always linking acclaim with wealth, he reported, "reputation in abundance is flowing in upon me which in the end will, with the Blessing of Providence, be wealth."[18] Indeed, by 1829 his portrait painting and teaching permitted him to pay off most of his debts and to collect enough advance commissions to sail again for Europe, where he studied and worked for nearly three years.[19]

He returned in 1832 with refreshed spirit and renewed hope for developing the support required to paint great paintings. With him he brought a partly finished painting of a *Gallery of the Louvre,* intended to instruct Americans who might never visit Paris. It succeeded well in capturing the essence of many masterpieces—in miniature. More central to his plan, he hoped to exhibit it profitably—but when tried that approach failed again dismally. Then the brightest opportunity yet to appear arose with the decision in 1837 to embellish Bulfinch's new Rotunda in the national Capitol with four giant historical canvases, each painted by a different artist. In Morse's mind, and indeed in the minds of his peers, there was little reason to doubt that he must be one of the four—but the congressional committee passed him by in a crushing blow to all of his dreams. He lost much more than the $10,000 commission, retiring to his bed from which he could see no hope through the blackness. Not even his friends' private subscription of $3,000 toward any painting he might choose to do roused him more than temporarily. His son Edward insisted that this disaster gave the "Death blow to his artistic ambition."[20]

It might not have been so except that another enthusiasm had already begun to capture him. Morse always believed that the "flash of genius" in which he conceived the idea of the telegraph occurred aboard the *Sully* during his 1832 return voyage to the United States. Under the impression that he was the first to whom the idea of the electric telegraph had occurred, he was able to describe the moment of conception as precisely as John Fitch had described his and to find fellow passengers who fully confirmed his memory. A shipboard conversation on Ampère's experiments with the electromagnet had led to the question of whether the speed of electricity was retarded by the length of the wire. Dr. Charles T. Jackson, Boston chemist and later claimant to the discovery of anesthesia, was in a position to reply. He responded that it was not, that electricity passed instantly over any length of wire.[21]

Morse immediately saw his vision and declared, "I see no reason why intelligence might not be instantaneously transmitted by electricity to any distance."[22] This he believed to be the true invention—although he later learned that others had seen substantially the same possibility before him and that experimentation with forms of an electric telegraph was even then under way.

His vision projected him into a culture that externally appeared altogether alien to that of the fine arts. Scientists and other experimenters were rapidly expanding the understanding of galvanic or current electricity, having moved on from the earlier studies that had been largely limited to static electricity. The first promising electric telegraph based on electrolysis appeared in 1809. In 1820 Ampère himself suggested that the Oersted effect, magnetism produced by an electric current, might be the basis for a magnetic needle telegraph. Both systems required improving the battery, and Volta's pile of alternating metallic and moist paper disks evolved into several forms of the wet cell. Another telegraphic possibility opened by Oersted's work applied the principle of the electromagnet. In Britain, William Sturgeon's dramatic success with electromagnets was recognized in 1825 by a premium of the Society of Arts. In the United States, Joseph Henry exceeded his results, lifting weights up to thirty-six hundred pounds and developing much better understanding of magnetic phenomena.

Morse came to electricity with some understanding of the field and with an awakened interest. Most recently, he had enjoyed the 1827 lectures on electromagnetism given by James Freeman Dana of Columbia College in the same New York Athenaeum series in which he had lectured.[23] But he did not bring the set of mind of a scientist and did not seek to study electricity as a science. He approached the telegraph as he had the steamboat, the water pump, and the marble-cutting machine, seeking to discover only enough of the principles involved to design a good, working system. The primary strength he brought to the telegraph was an excellent design capability based upon a mind practiced in forming and re-forming multiple elements into varying complexes. This sort of synthetic-spatial thinking is required in its most unalloyed form in painting or in sculpture where analytic, logical, verbal, or arithmetic thinking plays almost no role. Synthetic-spatial thinking is, of course, involved in most intellectual activity including science, but in technology it has to be central. Morse's mind was well practiced in this essential.

The balance of the ocean crossing he spent thinking about

a system composed of elements that his limited knowledge opened to him. He did not then explore the "state of the art": how to build the best battery, how to design the best electromagnet, or how best to insulate the wire; he asked himself the big questions. What form of intelligence, for example, was it possible to transmit by electricity? First he thought of transposing directly the kind of code used in the 1792 Chappe semaphore telegraph. Instead of different semaphore arm settings, each equated with a number and combinations of numbers keyed to words, Morse saw that he might transmit short bursts of electricity and longer bursts, separated by intervals between the bursts. He called the bursts dots and lines, later rendered as dots and dashes, and played around with different combinations that might stand for each number. The possibility of coding each letter in dots and dashes did occur to him, but the notebook in which he recorded his thoughts gives no evidence that he then experimented with letter coding.[24]

This form of intelligence transmission opened the way to the simplest possible circuitry. A single circuit would do, with some means for opening and closing it at one end and for detecting and reading or recording the signal at the other end. Thus he avoided the multiplication of circuits other telegraphic systems required, in some cases a separate circuit for each letter. How could the circuit be opened and closed, that is, the signal sent? Morse's surprising concept here was drawn from another, but related medium, printing. He sketched out individual pieces of type with flat and squared projections at the working surface.* The dot-dash code for each number could then be translated into corresponding teeth and spaces on the type, and the type might then be set in a composing stick (Morse used the term "portrule") to correspond with the coded words. By drawing a portrule of set type past a contact, the circuit would be opened and closed to transmit a sequence of coded dots and dashes.[25]

For the receiving end, Morse designed two alternate systems, both producing a written or recorded message—as anyone thinking in terms of printing and the printed word would first

* See page 118.

seek. One device advanced a roll of paper between a spark gap; each time a current passed it would leave a hole or a mark on the paper. In pursuing this idea, Morse consulted Charles T. Jackson, and his fellow passenger suggested that tumeric paper dipped in sulfate of soda might produce the desired discoloration at the point where the current passed.[26]

Morse's second design for a recorder embraced the same roll of paper advanced by clockwork, but in place of the spark gap he substituted an electromagnet that would actuate a lever to move a pen or pencil across the paper whenever the circuit was closed. Jackson may have contributed more here, too, than Morse was willing to concede when the chemist later claimed to have invented the telegraph himself. Jackson had introduced into shipboard discussion the recent experiments of Ampère in electromagnetism, and Morse's notebook contains an unambiguous sketch of the Pixii generator Ampère had first demonstrated only the month before the *Sully* sailed. Immediately after his return, Jackson published an account of the device in the *American Journal of Science,* so unless Morse had another source of information, too, his sketch probably came from Jackson.[27] The function of the Pixii magnet opposed in the sketch by a rotating permanent magnet was of course to produce electricity, but Morse's sketch of it was almost identical with his drawing, three pages further on, of the magnet in his telegraph.

Morse's shipboard sketches, recorded in a small notebook, display graphically the character of his thinking. They show his ability to conceptualize all the elements of a complete telegraphic system and to design alternative components. They reveal at this stage no input of analytic science or projected circuit parameters and quantitative performance. Indeed, they resemble remarkably the spatial images recorded in his travel notebooks of the scenes, costumes, and technology he encountered.

Morse had reason to congratulate himself upon having designed an electromagnetic telegraph before the ship docked— even though he had given little attention to the materials or manner of construction of the electrical components. To his brothers, he spilled over with enthusiasm, convincing Sidney that, at last, fortune might be within their grasp. He immediately launched into attempts to cast the coded type and to make the other components required by his design. He did the work himself, despite his deficiency in manual skill that he always acknowledged, because he lacked the funding to contract the work to competent artisans who might have been able to improvise enough to make the system work. Still worse, he had barely begun the long course of required development when he had to stop. His time was urgently required to provide an immediate income to support himself and his children, who had been parceled out among his relatives at the time of his wife's death.[28]

Much as he deplored portrait painting as mere hackwork, he did return to it in this need and stayed with it even after he gave up his hope of painting grand historical canvases. Not unwillingly, he became engulfed in controversy in defense of the National Academy of Design, and, voluntarily, he entered city politics. Twice he was defeated for mayor, running on nativist tickets in 1836 and 1841, but overwhelming defeats never entirely extinguished his political activity as they finally did his art.[29]

After declining an appointment at West Point, he accepted one at New York University that proved critical to his difficult shift of careers. His initial appointment to the Chair of Painting and Sculpture coincided almost exactly with his return to New York, but he did not become active in the university until the new Gothic building on Washington Square was occupied in 1835. Morse then moved in, renting the top room in the northwest tower and five rooms on the floor below. He made the university his residence and brought with him his own students whose tuition represented the only university income he received. By then he had also changed his title to accord with the terminology worked out so carefully for the National Academy; then and thereafter he was listed as professor of the literature of the arts of design.[30]

In the new building, Morse established a studio that impressed one of his students in its similarities to a research laboratory. He instructed, studied colors and methods, and developed ordered approaches to the attainment of good painting techniques. His students regarded him as the major figure in the New York art world and perhaps in America, and some of them, such as Daniel Huntington and William Page, went on to successful careers. Yet almost immediately Morse became more and more absorbed with the telegraphic apparatus that he also moved into his quarters. This his students tolerated, knowing that it could lead nowhere, but they also felt saddened that so fine a painter was being deflected from his important life work.[31]

Morse was not wrong in insisting in later years that the telegraph was achieved within the walls of the university. First of all, he found there the space he had not had since returning to America where he could spread out his batteries, wires, and instruments, leave them for days, and then return to make changes and try again. He also found the opportunity for extended contemplation he had not enjoyed at his brothers' homes or in roominghouses. Then, gradually, he became part of a community that was not uncongenial to him and that offered needed help. Initially, he was embarrassed to "expose to ridicule" his rude and ineffective apparatus as the sole fruit of "so many hours of laborious thought."[32]

Leonard D. Gale, professor of geology and mineralogy, was the first to help substantially. By the time he examined the telegraph, in January 1836, Morse had provided dot-dash coding for each letter and had abandoned a melodeonlike keyboard transmitter, which today might be thought of as similar to a typewriter keyboard, to return to the portrule he had conceived on the *Sully*. Still, it remained crude and would not function through more than forty feet of wire. Gale saw immediately some of the problems: only a single-cell battery was being used and very few loops of wire around the magnetic core. Through much of the next year, Gale worked with Morse preparing magnets, winding wire, and constructing batteries. Gale knew that an "intensity" battery was required, a battery of several cells connected in series to get higher voltage, and that this must be connected with a magnet of a hundred or more loops. When the two men coupled a twenty-cell battery to a many-loop magnet, they were ultimately able to send the signal through ten miles of wire, Morse's stated goal.[33]

Gale had used electricity in his research and had worked with Joseph Henry in one experimental inquiry.[34] He had also read and he referred Morse to Henry's important 1831 article that had been the basis of his improvement of the telegraph. Henry's insights, achieved prior to a distinct understanding of Ohm's law, were essential to Morse's success.[35]

Morse made Gale a partner, and, in September 1837 acquired a second partner from within the university community. Alfred Vail had graduated in 1836 and became excited by the prospect of the telegraph. He seems to have decided to throw his efforts in with Morse after learning of Morse's apparently independent invention of the relay—Henry had certainly developed it earlier, although Gale credited it to Morse. This was a device for using an electromagnet to close a second circuit containing its own independent battery, and thus extending the range of the telegraph. Vail offered to finance the construction of the instruments required for a trial of the telegraph, the money to come from his father, who owned the Speedwell Ironworks in Morristown, New Jersey. Vail himself possessed considerable mechanical ability, which he demonstrated in improving the instruments and in devising such changes as the substitution of a stylus for a pen in the recording instrument.[36]

Sometime after Gale improved Morse's battery and magnet and before Vail made the new instruments, the surviving canvas-stretcher telegraph was altered to its present condition.* Symbolically, it united the two cultures of Samuel F. B. Morse, its most conspicuous component being a painter's canvas stretcher. This constituted his receiver; within this available form, he incorporated the magnetic, recording device he had visualized aboard the *Sully*. Whenever the transmitter turned on the current, the magnet pulled a lever, moving a pen or pencil across a slowly rotating tape. The tape was advanced by clockwork scavenged from a spring-wound clock.[37]

Morse's transmitter, too, incorporated the concepts he had sketched in 1832. In this case the external form he adapted was a familiar printer's composing stick, converted into a movable portrule set with type, one piece for each letter. As

* See page 120.

the portrule was cranked manually past a contacting lever, the sawtooth type opened and closed the circuit to produce a sequence of dots and dashes.

By this time, Morse was ready to seek approval of his telegraph and its introduction to use. The three partners agreed to answer Secretary of the Treasury Levi Woodbury's invitation for telegraph proposals made earlier in 1837. He of course had in mind semaphore telegraphs, but Morse felt that his was much preferable and filed a caveat with the commissioner of patents on his invention. The system was formally demonstrated in January 1838 at the Speedwell Ironworks and to an invited group at New York University. Another logical forum in the city would have been the Mechanics Institute to which both Gale and Vail belonged, but its fairs were held in the summer and its regular conversational meetings were not appropriate. The summer fair concentration of the American Institute probably also ruled out that institution, although Morse later exhibited with them and received their gold medal.[38]

Instead, Morse took Vail with him in February to a presentation in Washington, stopping on the way at the Franklin Institute in Philadelphia. That organization's committee on science and the arts was very enthusiastic in its commendation of "Professor Morse" and urged him on to further trials.[39] In Washington, Morse demonstrated the telegraph to President Van Buren and his cabinet and, at another session, to the House Committee on Commerce. The committee chairman, F. O. J. Smith of Maine, was so enthusiastic that he offered to become a partner in return for handling European affairs and for his expertise in American politics. In one of the most clear-cut cases of conflict of interest on record, the new partner quickly offered a House bill granting $30,000 to conduct a long-distance trial—although he then absented himself, officially, from the House. The other partners, dubious from the start, were increasingly alienated by Smith's lack of principle, self-seeking, and undependability. His nickname, "Fog" Smith, turned out to be a relatively benign epithet.[40]

Yet this was no more than grit in the machinery, and Morse began to feel that he might hope for the early realization of

the great personal and public advantages implicit in the telegraph. His best hope was that the government would buy and
operate it as a public utility; he saw it as a much speedier and
improved mail system. The partners would be compensated,
and the people of the nation would be the beneficiaries. He
saw parallel possibilities in Europe both for compensation and
for still wider public benefits, and he eagerly accompanied
"Fog" Smith on a transatlantic trip that, however, revealed only
long and rocky roads. In England, Morse's patent application
was turned off abruptly, although individual Englishmen,
including his leading competitor, Charles Wheatstone, were
remarkably friendly. In France a patent was easy enough to
obtain, and Morse won as well the plaudits of the Académie
des Sciences, but no more funding appeared than on the other
side of the Channel. An agent was sent to Eastern Europe
where the single nibble, from Russia, faded away to nothing.[41]

For Morse it was largely a lost year except for his exciting
meeting with his fellow artist—and inventor—L. J. M. Daguerre. The knowledge he took home about photography was
not enough to reduce his unhappiness at discovering that
neither the Congress nor his partners were doing anything at
all with the telegraph. Still, the new art was remarkably
interesting to the portraitist-inventor—and it might add to
his interim income from painting and teaching. Morse had
Daguerre elected to the National Academy, and he began to
work with the new science professor who came to the university
after Leonard Gale left in 1838, John William Draper, professor
of chemistry and botany. Draper succeeded first in making a
daguerreotype portrait, the object of greatest importance to
Morse, and together they established a glass-roofed studio on
top of the Washington Square building where they could take
maximum advantage of the sunlight. After such success as
reducing the exposure time to about sixty seconds, Draper
withdrew, but Morse went on to teach photographic portraiture
to eager learners, including such leaders of the emerging
profession as Mathew Brady.[42]

The telegraph remained his primary quest, and Morse
elicited from Joseph Henry an enthusiastic response. The
scientist declared in 1839 that he believed "science was now

ripe for the application" and that Morse's plan involved "no difficulties in the way but such as ingenuity and enterprise may obviate." By 1842 he was ready to agree that Morse's system was superior to any of the competing telegraphs familiar to him. He was genuinely anxious to see Morse succeed because he took pride in American technological achievements and was eager to see science applied to technology. He believed that science could predict what was possible in technology and what was not.[43]

Henry was a help to Morse, both in specifics and in the use Morse made of his favorable view in gaining support, but the later estrangement between the two men was a direct function of their different understanding of the relationships between science and technology. Henry believed that the role of science was to make discoveries and that a mature science opened the door to practical applications that would be achieved as soon as society was ready to put through the technological change. Inventors were "men of action," accessory to scientists, who were "men of mind." Morse much resented the view that invention and work with technology were things other and less than intellectual activity. He was convinced that all of his work was based upon thought.[44]

Henry's rigid view of science was commonly held by the other leaders with whom he worked in trying to professionalize American science and bring it to new standards of rigor. It led him to disdain commercial gain from inventions but to become furious when credit for the science behind them was withheld. On that account he was outraged when Vail and Morse pointedly failed to acknowledge his role accurately in 1846, and Morse behaved even more badly in reaction.[45]

Morse's view of invention and science was more warped than Henry's and in different directions. He valued science and sought to obtain its best insights when needed and to gain the help and good opinion of scientists. Although he knew that his work with the telegraph was almost wholly something other than scientific inquiry, he sometimes misrepresented his role. He had a fine sensitivity on how best to advance his own interests, clinging tenaciously, for example, to the title of "professor" without bothering to make clear that his academic field was art. Many of his European predecessors and competitors in electric telegraphy held scientific professorships—Professor Soemmerring, Professor Steinheil, Professor Weber, and Professor Wheatstone among them—and Morse felt elevated to be regarded as a member of this community. In his controversy with Henry, he revealed a readiness, on occasion, to distort the truth consciously. But he did understand better than many the intellectual creativity required to realize the telegraph, something different from and beyond the science involved.

Over several years, Morse and his colleagues worked on numerous trials, experiments, and designs—although at a very uneven rate. He was nearly always hobbled for funding. A concentrated development effort and an extended trial were imperative, but Morse might have attained neither without the large outside support finally provided by Congress. In 1840 Morse patented the telegraph, but only after rejecting Wheatstone's offer that they pool their endeavors and after Wheatstone took out his own U.S. patent.[46] In 1842 Morse again petitioned Congress for funding, now that the mood in Washington seemed less negative than it had through the depth of the panic. Morse was helped by Ellsworth and a new colleague at the university, Professor James C. Fisher. New Washington demonstrations went well and good responses were received, but the seemingly endless waiting stretched again into months. Finally on March 3, 1843, the act was signed granting Morse $30,000 for a trial of his telegraph between Washington and Baltimore.[47]

The most intense period of development followed this grant. With money in his hands Morse succeeded in reactivating his partners, appointing Gale, Vail, and Fisher assistant superintendents, and finding that even Smith returned to seek some of the contracting profits. Vail again undertook to get the instruments fabricated as Morse kept thinking up new designs and directing him to new trials. Vail reported that Morse, from beginning to end, invented more forms of transmitter than of any other component, and the process of simplification showed more clearly here than anywhere else. By the time of the trial, the portrule, whether straight, circular, cranked, or keyed, was given up for a manual key that became known as the "Morse key."[48] Recent tests at the Smithsonian Institution have revealed that the limiting factor in the original telegraph was the portrule—which could do no more than six words a minute. The key easily tripled that speed. Under Morse's direction, Vail carried out experimental trials with batteries and magnets as well.[49]

However, Morse turned to Draper to help him obtain answers to a long-standing worry that Henry had reinforced, agreeing that the Morse telegraph was "adequate for short distances but that something more might be needed for long runs." He meant something more than the relay or the voltage and magnetic field increase that Gail had achieved. In August 1843, Morse, advised by Draper, conducted tests over 160 miles of wire and using a 48-cell battery. He got a good plot of the drop in current as the resistance, in the form of a longer wire, was increased. Morse's report, and Draper's analytical interpretation concluding that a long-line telegraph was possible, were published in the *American Journal of Science*.[50]

The actual construction of the line from Washington to Baltimore was a continuing learning experience, most of it unplanned. The whole process was difficult precisely because there was no significant pool of electrical technology to draw upon. Morse had learned that he did not need two wires to complete the circuit but could ground his system and use the earth for the return. He did not, however, know how to construct the line economically, and the initial decision to bury insulated wire encased in lead pipes turned out to be wrong. A patent pipe was contracted for, and Smith made one of his few positive contributions in bringing Ezra Cornell into the enterprise at this point. Cornell was a roving plow salesman with a contriving mind that led him to design a plow on the spot that would open the ground, lay the lead pipe, and close the trench in one operation.[51]

By the time contracting, personal, and personnel problems were overcome and nine miles of encased wire laid, $23,000 of the $30,000 had been spent. Then only was it discovered that the wire in the pipe shorted out uncontrollably and that there was no way to insulate it satisfactorily. Both Henry and Cornell urged stringing uninsulated wire on poles—an old idea—but apparently Charles G. Page, examiner in the Patent Office, was the first to try to convince Morse of it. This solution worked well, the unneeded pipe was sold, and the wire already on hand was applied to the task. The line was completed within the appropriation.[52]

It was complete from Washington to Annapolis Junction by May 1, 1844, when the Whig party National Convention met in Baltimore. Morse made the most of a dramatic opportunity by stationing Vail at Annapolis Junction to telegraph news to him in Washington as soon as received by train from Baltimore. He thus was able to break to the sitting Congress word of the Clay-Frelinghuysen ticket—word very quickly confirmed when the train got to town. The first message over the completed line from Washington to Baltimore was sent on May 24, "What hath God wrought?" opening the way to still further drama when the Democratic Convention met in Baltimore the following day. Morse in this case was able to report to Congress the unexpected nomination of Polk and to the convention the unexpected declination of the vice-presidential nominee, Silas Wright.[53] Now at last the telegraph was a success before the world. Surely the obvious benefits would follow and the fortune Morse always sought seemed within reach.

Even then, nothing came to him automatically. After the agonizing difficulties of designing and redesigning the telegraph, of painfully pursuing the Congress, and of fighting on all fronts to put the trial system together, Morse was anxious to sell the telegraph to Congress and withdraw. Of course, Smith urged him to hold on to it in the conviction that he would make much more money. Yet making the most money he could had never been Morse's goal; he wanted the status and the competent wealth he felt recognition as the "inventor" of the telegraph deserved. He wanted a degree of security, no longer to have to "live by his wits." He recalled that the French parliament had provided an appropriate model in awarding to Daguerre a fine, lifetime pension. That much he felt he deserved, but in addition be believed that the best social use of the telegraph called for government ownership and operation.[54]

He therefore plotted a new course designed to permit him

to withdraw from the immediate frictions of planning and management while the government purchase was pursued. He readily accepted Amos Kendall's offer to take over these tasks he so disliked. Kendall, an astute and honest man, had been a member of Andrew Jackson's "kitchen cabinet" and then postmaster general. Vail and Gale followed Morse's lead and made Kendall agent for their two and one shares, against Morse's nine, but Smith held out with his four shares. After Congress voted $8,000 to permit Morse to run the telegraph for a year, Kendall gave one more try at selling the telegraph to the government.[55]

When he, too, failed, he turned to the founding of a network of companies to build and operate lines, most of them radiating out of New York. Generally, half of the stock was sold to raise the needed capital and the rest retained by the four patentees. On this basis, the Magnetic Telegraph Company was formed on May 15, 1845, to build the line from New York to Philadelphia, and others followed, providing links from New York to Boston, New York to Buffalo, Philadelphia to Pittsburgh, and Washington to Mobile. The traffic rose slowly on the early lines, but it was enough to extend a handsome promise. Brokers, lottery agents, various businessmen, and newspapers began to realize their great need for instant communication.[56]

The networks were filled in amid financial conflict, patent suits, and a continuing evolution of the technology. The telegraph that came to prevail in the United States and most of the world was founded on the simple, durable system contrived by Morse and those he had called to his aid. Some of the changes grew, unexpectedly, out of experience; for example, the larger American telegraph offices soon turned to simple sounders in place of the more complicated recording receivers. The operators could write down what they heard faster than they could transcribe the tapes—although at the same time printing or recording receivers based on the work of competitors were widely adopted. Duplexing, or sending two messages simultaneously, was discovered early by Morse but did not become practicable for some time. Page worked on the design of an electric generator for Morse's telegraph, but that, too, awaited further development. The crossing of large rivers posed a problem, only partly solved by stringing wires from very high poles or sending the messages across by boat. A satisfactory solution depended upon the use of gutta-percha and the development of cables. That development opened the prospect of crossing still broader waters—including the Atlantic Ocean.[57]

Morse found a fine method for converting his patent right ' into income, as a major shareholder in several companies. He became a wealthy man; he no longer had to feel outdistanced by his publisher brother, Sidney, who had been listed at least since 1842 as worth $100,000. Morse reported in 1853 a ten-year telegraph income of $193,000, most of it during the preceding three years—and it continued to grow. In 1858, ten European nations awarded Morse 400,000 francs in recognition of the value of his telegraph to their countries; the fact that only a small part came to him personally was not a problem. He maintained fine homes in the city and near Poughkeepsie, married a second time, and visited Europe frequently as he had always hoped to do—now with a numerous retinue.[58]

The motivation behind Morse's achievement stands out in his history. In his pursuit of art and in the telegraph, he conducted crusades for the benefit of his country and of mankind—both designed to achieve as well his own enrichment. Like Rumsey, Fitch, Fulton, and most of the inventor-projectors of the era, he sought recognition and personal profit without any dissimulation. This was not a character defect but a part of the life of the time, encouraged by the patent system and by the models and values surrounding the prevailing concept of invention.

But what Morse had wrought is not to be understood as a function simply of drive and entrepreneurial capacity. Intermittently, he had great energy and drive and he was effective in organizing and moving men, but his most important capacity was far closer to the heart of the technological enterprise. He possessed an ability to think well spatially that he turned to the contrivance of machines and telegraphic systems, first in his mind, then often on paper, then in reality. He had used the same sort of thinking in his painting, where he combined it with highly developed skills of hand and eye, a combination he never achieved in mechanical technology and electrical instrumentation. Vail and Smith, in fact, complained of his mechanical ineptitude, and Vail regarded it as a significant failing that he was not even a good telegraph operator. His success with the telegraph did not rest upon the kind of fingertip knowledge of which some inventors boasted.

His great strength remained a quality of mind that permitted him to manipulate mental images of three-dimensional telegraph components as well as complete telegraphic systems, altering them at will and projecting various possibilities for change and development. Although he had used this mode of thinking in his art, his telegraph in no way depended upon his art. Conspicuous success in each, however, absolutely required conspicuous ability in spatial thinking.

- 5 -

Morse Images:
A Pictorial Essay

Figure 40. Morse self-portrait, circa 1809

Figure 41. Watercolor of the Morse family, circa 1810

THE EXTENSIVE visual imagery associated with Samuel F. B. Morse offers a fine opportunity to move through his art career and through his telegraph career as well, by way of images. Already in his day the record of a leading artist who played a major role in developing a science-based technology had to be explained. The one approach that ties together these two apparently diverse careers, other than bare coincidence, is the perception of that mental manipulation of images that lay at the center of each effort.

Morse's delicate self-portrait is a miniature on ivory done during his college years while he was painting miniatures of friends and townspeople as a source of needed income. Like other painting, portraiture required him to combine the elementary images he saw with those he remembered into a composition that, unavoidably, represented an interpretation. Even more was his contemporaneous watercolor of his family a composition of familiar mental images combined with what he could see visually at a single setting.

Figure 42. The Dying Hercules, 1812,
sculpture produced as a study for the painting

LONDON

Morse's London years were dedicated to study and studio work, the objective of which was to become a truly great artist producing great canvases that would interpret historical and mythological episodes. The death of Hercules was an ideal subject that he pursued with vigor and, to a point, success. His sculpture was recognized immediately by the Society of Arts in its award of a gold medal, and it has been recognized by critics since as possessing integrity and effectiveness. The elements are harmonized to convey feeling. It was a promising beginning.

Its application to a painting for which it was a study won more muted praise. It was submitted in competition to the Royal Academy of Art where it received no award, although

Figure 43. The Dying Hercules, 1813

it did gain favorable notice in the press. Recent commentators have been less kind but more accurate in regarding the painting as a failure, lumpy in its effect. The details, or components, are at least as good as in the sculpture, but somehow they do not work together to convey the strength in extreme adversity the sculpture projects. He did not succeed in translating the spatial imagery of the sculpture into a good, two-dimensional/painting.

Figure 44. Benjamin Silliman, 1825   *Figure 45. James Kent, 1823*

PORTRAITS

In retrospect, Morse's art reached its highest level in portraiture, even though he never held that branch of painting in high esteem. At the very beginning of his effort at painting, he turned to portraiture because he could earn money by painting portraits as he could not from any other form of painting. Years of study with the best teachers, travel to the art centers of the West, and unremitting effort never changed the truth of that initial discovery. He kept returning to portrait painting as a means of livelihood when one stratagem after another failed to disclose any other continuing source of income. As he persevered in that pursuit, his skill grew until he stood in the forefront of American portraitists of his day.

A minimal level of skill was essential for commercial success; likenesses had to satisfy patrons both in accuracy and in attractiveness. Morse achieved much more, especially in interpreting and depicting personality and character. He followed the custom of including identifying props: mineral specimens,

Figure 46.
The Muse—Susan Walker Morse, 1837

Figure 47.
The Marquis de Lafayette, 1825

lecture notes, and a watch for Silliman; a copybook, comfortable surroundings, and a contemplative sky for Susan; and busts of Washington and Franklin and a pyrotechnic sky for Lafayette. However, in Morse's case, these were labels directing attention to the pictured individual.

When he painted his teacher and friend, Benjamin Silliman, he brought both spatial images and emotional memories. The Silliman of the portrait is a warm, communicative man who looks out and through the viewer with specific knowledge but enlightened understanding. Chancellor Kent led Morse to remark that he could not paint an impatient man. Of course he could not; spatial thinking calls for untrammeled concentration, and he had no alternative but to show Kent as an impatient man with no very favorable attributes. Of Susan, his daughter, he showed many images: small girl, grown woman, and bright, determined individual. Lafayette, as sometimes assessed, may represent his highest achievement; he somehow projected the dash of youth and the majesty of progress through turbulent times of a now elderly man.

Figure 48. The Old House Chamber in the Capitol, 1823

GRAND CANVASES

Morse's *Old House Chamber in the Capitol* represents his greatest effort to attain his ideal in art by presenting an ennobling theme, in this case, a patriotic theme. It was a masterpiece of spatial thinking based upon the difficult composition of the separate portrait studies he had made of each congressman within a complex space lighted unsatisfactorily. The perspective was so difficult that he had to repaint the hall several times. He had to compromise with the real world in order to get something of the face of every congressman, despite the circular seating and central lighting. One of the images he brought with him, of his father, he placed in the balcony.

*Figure 49. Allegorical Landscape
Showing New York University, 1837*

Morse occupied his rooms in the new Gothic building on Washington Square in 1835, and in 1837 he painted the New York University building in an imagined, Italianate landscape. This has not been evaluated by art critics as one of his masterpieces, but it is an achievement in imaginative, spatial thinking. The placement of the university in an Italian scene represents a mode of celebration that came very easily to Morse, who so admired the Italy he experienced in his travels. In 1837 he was remembering particularly his trip of 1830 and 1831 when he filled his notebooks with little drawings of details and of scenes, and his mind with images he could not forget.

Figure 50. Interior of the Convent of S. Benedetto, 1831

ITALIAN IMAGES

Morse's travel notebooks were filled with spatial images, some of them translated into words but many rendered in small pencil sketches. Most of his sketches were of details or components, and some of these he sought out specifically, for example, to provide the images he would need in a projected

Figure 51. Italian sketches, 1831

painting of Columbus. Often, he was thinking of a larger composition into which the details would be fitted. Sometimes he sketched an entire scene—but seldom with the attention he gave to the Convent of S. Benedetto. Usually he recorded only architectural components, details of scenes, or elements of costume next to technological or material details—such as the rudder, mantilla, and vanes.

His observations upon an Italian ax demonstrate his sensitivity to the essence of technology. He commented that if the Americans had used Italian axes, they would never have cleared the continent. He was right; the elegant American ax was capable of felling trees three times as fast as the unbalanced European ax.

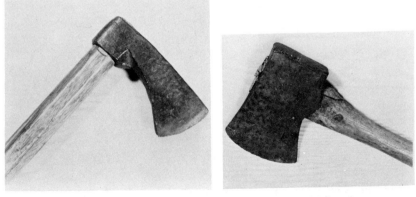

Figure 52. A European ax   *Figure 53. An American ax*

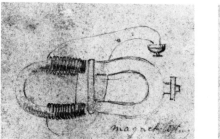

Figure 54.
Pixii generator

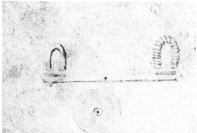

Figure 55.
Recording telegraph with electromagnet

THE 1832 NOTEBOOK TELEGRAPH

During his return voyage from Europe in 1832, Morse sketched designs for the major components of a working, electric telegraph system. He seems to have begun his electromagnetic version of the telegraph with the Pixii generator and to have applied his image of this directly to a recording telegraph actuated by a similarly conceived electromagnet. He envisaged at the same time a mechanically cranked transmitter in the form of a portrule set with coded type. The type, one for each number, at this stage, made and broke the circuit as it was cranked past a contact.

Figure 56. Coded type

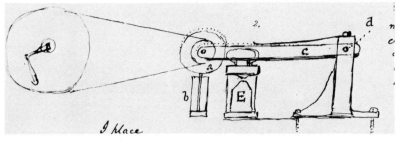

Figure 57. Type line cutter, 1848

CONTINUING TELEGRAPH DESIGNS

Morse followed this practice of sketching out his mental images and conceptions at each point thereafter when he returned to the continuing development of the telegraph. His letters to Vail are especially rich in sketched imagery to illustrate directions for new trials, experiments, or instruments. Vail's corresponding notebooks also contain visual imagery. At times, Morse turned out a continuing succession of inventive ideas, such as this machine for cutting a line of coded type following a keyed message. His telegraph line test terminals were well conceived.

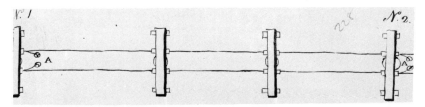

Figure 58. Telegraph line with continuity test terminals, 1848

Figure 59. The canvas-stretcher telegraph, 1837

THE CANVAS-STRETCHER TELEGRAPH

The canvas-stretcher telegraph preserved in the National Museum of American History is the telegraph Morse had in hand when he filed his 1837 caveat. It represents, almost precisely, a fulfillment of designs he had sketched in his 1832 notebook. Its physical form, of course, might have been grossly different; this was largely determined by the use of the canvas stretcher. Canvas stretchers, next to paints, brushes, and canvas,

Figure 60. The telegraph portrule, 1837

Figure 61. A printer's composing stick

were the painter's most essential equipment; Morse used one because it was there.

By this time, he had provided dot-dash coding for each letter and pieces of type corresponding to each coded letter. The type was set sequentially to spell out words and placed in the portrule, coded teeth up. When the hand crank was turned, the coded type moved the right end of the lever arm up and down, making and breaking electrical contact to send the encoded message. The type was made of lead or brass, the image out of which the portrule had been conceived clearly coming from printer's type set in a composing stick.

Although Morse designed many different transmitters or senders, he kept coming back to the portrule principle—even after the hand key had proved its initial superiority. The electromagnetic basis of the receiver-recorder did not change, even the substitution of a sounder for a recording tape representing a detail.

Figure 62. Morse key, 1844

THE 1844 TELEGRAPH

The introduction of the Morse telegraph was not assured until the successful May 24, 1844, Washington-Baltimore trial, funded by the $30,000 congressional development grant. The telegraph system differed in many respects from Morse's 1832 designs, from his 1837 system, and even from his 1840 patent designs. It was the product of an evolution based upon a multitude of mental conceptions, many of which were tested at least in part. Morse was the most prolific generator of these concepts, but Vail, Gale, and Cornell made important contributions, and ideas were assimilated from other telegraph projectors and from scientific studies.

The instruments used in the 1844 trial were made by Alfred Vail, and they bear the impress of his ingenuity. The key, which became known as the "Morse key," was signed by him, lending support to later assertions that Vail had invented it. He did not claim this, however, although possibly impeded by an agreement to pool all improvements under the Morse patent. Continuing inventiveness was involved in every step of telegraph development, and much of it cannot be decisively attributed to a single individual.

Figure 63. Replica of the 1844 recorder

Morse, of course, always believed that he invented the telegraph in 1832. For some purposes, 1844 is a more meaningful date; then the Morse telegraph system reached a point of immediate applicability and utility.

Figure 64. Tape with recorded message, 1844

Figure 65. Morse's Society of Arts medal, 1813

EMULATION

Medals awarded for excellence symbolize the ancient process of emulation, or encouragement through competition against the best models. Morse's Society of Arts medal, awarded at an early stage of his art career for his sculpture of *The Dying Hercules*, constituted a helpful encouragement to exertion and further competitive effort. His American Institute medal was awarded in 1842 when Morse's hopes of Congressional support were rising but before the grant was made.

Figure 66. Morse's American Institute medal, 1842

Figure 67. Christian Schussele, Men of Progress, 1862

Still, the parallel encouragement by emulation of both Morse's painting and his telegraph was more than a hangover from a bygone age. The concept of emulation remained significant because it addressed the processes of thinking and of creativity which had deep and common similarities in the fine and the mechanical arts.

By Morse's day, technological emulation was most practiced in holding up the inventor, rather than the invention, as the model for emulation. Each popular invention was tied to an eponymic inventor, and inventors were, indeed, raised to the level of popular heroes. Christian Schussele's 1862 painting raised Morse to the highest pinnacle, as an inventor to be emulated.

- 6 -

The Contriving Mind

MORSE AND Fulton were accorded places in the American pantheon of inventors, to which Fitch was often admitted as well. Morse himself had grown up with Franklin, Fulton, and Whitney as inventor models to be emulated, and after the telegraph he quickly attained similar stature. Schussele's 1862 painting surrounded him with such contemporary inventors as Goodyear, Colt, and McCormick but Morse was assigned the place of honor. The inventor-heroes were credited with new machines that before them had not existed; the prosperity and happiness of America was understood to be based upon, and each day further advanced by, such inventions.[1]

The need to find an eponym for each technological change was given legal sanction by the patent system, but it had a more complex basis. Governments had long been personified by their chiefs of state, armies by their generals, and churches by their pontiffs. The association of a single individual with each major innovation had an additional root that grew more specifically out of the technological process itself; this was emulation. Just as the best work was held up to the apprentice as a model, so invention might be encouraged by holding up as models the best inventors.

The process of invention was thus grossly simplified, but in socially positive directions. It may be a reflection of our current malaise that good scholars today see "technological change" as primarily "a problem-solving activity."[2] Certainly problems were not the emphasis of those responsible for the steamboat and the telegraph. Instead, they were overwhelmed by the scope for applying new machines to so rich a continent and so wide a world. Fitch saw many ways in which steam might be applied to transportation, whether by land or by water. Fulton believed that he could build a machine that would make him rich and famous because, by then, he knew how. Morse certainly did not begin with a problem crying out for the solution of instantaneous communication; he began with the possibility of combining electromagnetism and the long-distance transmission of electric current to a useful application. None of these men invented what they asserted or what their patents proclaimed, but they all deserved the celebration they received—for their direct contributions to technological change and for the influence their example had on others.[3]

Inventiveness was, of course, responsive to needs, but it often looked for the need after a possible invention had arisen in the mind. Biological evolution offers an interesting parallel. Natural selection gives a preference to those individuals best adapted to the needs of their environment—but the genetic change comes first. Positive mutations are selected for perpetuation; just as inventive ideas may be selected for development when they prove applicable to social and economic needs—or even when such needs can be aroused. Darwin solved his greatest problem, "the species question," that is, the question of major change, by postulating a process of minor variation and positive selection.

Inventiveness is a constant accompaniment of machine technology, just as individual variation is a constant feature of all life. The variation in components as well as in the design of the whole machine was extensive in the cases of the steamboat and the telegraph before either was put into effective operation. After that accomplishment, the numbers of identifiable inventions continued and actually increased until each machine reached a plateau of matured effectiveness. This cumulative process could produce genuinely "new" machines—called by some "strategic inventions."

The patent system conditioned men's views of invention while at the same time it was altered to conform better to their anticipations. The initial Patent Law of 1790 did not work as had been hoped. Most of the sixty-seven patents granted under it were inconsequential, although a few were important. Eli Whitney always bemoaned the injustice he suffered under his cotton gin patent, not conceding that a part of the problem was his own. Oliver Evans fought an uphill struggle, too, for his automated flourmill, with dubious personal advantage. The steamboat patents, of course, benefited neither the patentees nor society, and their failure had led Fulton and Livingston to rely instead on the New York State monopoly. The federal examining process proved so harrowing and unsuccessful that the 1793 law substituted a system of mere registration, the patentees having then to rely completely on the courts to defend their rights.[4]

This, too, was a failure, finally superseded in 1836 by a law that established a formal Patent Office and provided for the award of patents to recognize novelty, originality, and utility. Conflict and court battles continued, but confidence in patents returned, and the number awarded annually rapidly increased. Morse decided to file his 1837 caveat at just this point, and the ensuing patent held, providing a firm foundation for the rapid extension of a national telegraph system and bringing Morse his fortune.

There was much that was unreal about patents and even more about the cadre of lawyers, judges, patent firms, and periodicals that grew up around the Patent Office. Since most inventions required a period of research and development to bring them to effectiveness, a major need remained unfulfilled. How could the inventor finance the required study, trial, and modification? A valid patent did not make such funding available to Morse any more than an ethereal patent had helped Fitch. One proposed solution was to go back to the premium system that had long preceded the enactment of the first patent act.

Thomas Ewbank, who succeeded Morse's friend Ellsworth as Patent Office commissioner, proposed the creation of a $100,000 Inventor's Premium Fund out of the annual fees collected by the Patent Office. Cash awards and medals named for Franklin, Whitney, and Fulton would be given for particularly worthy inventions, helping to encourage their development. To administer these premiums, he suggested a board of members appointed by the Congress and the president and of representatives of the leading mechanics institutes in Boston, New York, Philadelphia, Baltimore, and Charleston.[5]

This was the emulation approach; it harked back to the 1791 French fund of 300,000 livres awarded for inventions in the useful arts that included the still older Society of Arts restriction against patenting winning inventions. There was never any chance that Ewbank's proposal could be wedded to the patent system. The two approaches were nowhere successfully combined, although in the United States emulation rose again beside the revivified patent system. Multitudes of premiums were awarded at the agricultural fairs now held throughout the country and especially at the annual or biennial industrial fairs in the major cities. New machines of many sorts were entered in competition and put on display in the hope of selling them, and Americans flocked to enjoy them and to have their faith renewed in the beneficence of technological advance.[6]

Both the patent and the premium systems gave what amounted to terminal awards for machine invention or improvement and therefore did not have to confront directly the inventive process or the manner in which mechanical creativity functioned. Some sense of that process was perceived by all who worked constructively with invention. Realities of the process, too, constituted at least a part of the training and educational efforts that multiplied as machine technology spread. Mechanics institutes, lyceums, and various societies usually incorporated the model system of instruction and stimulation in their programs, chiefly through fairs and exhibitions. Several of the mechanics institutes established repositories of machines to instruct and motivate mechanics and inventors. Often more conspicuous were the classes launched by the institutes and lyceums in general education and in the elementary sciences closest to mechanisms.

Engineering programs supplied similar approaches at a higher level, from West Point and Rensselaer to the Lawrence and Sheffield schools at Harvard and Yale. In the latter schools, the intentions of the founders to improve technology by teaching the useful arts were sidetracked by faculties that instead pursued their own researches in basic science. New York University's initial motto, "Perstando et Praestando Util-

♦

itate," characterized emulation in the useful arts, but its later generalization to "Perstare et Praestare" eliminated the emphasis on useful knowledge and paralleled acceptance of the standard classical curriculum. The realities of mechanical creativity were masked over time and again by deeply ingrained philosophies of education and by the vibrant ambitions of the science community.[7]

On the other hand, the American attachment to a good elementary education proved an immense advantage in developing mechanical technology. American mechanics, especially in New England and the Middle States, were generally literate and at home in arithmetic, some geometry, and trigonometry. Acute foreign observers related American adaptiveness and inventiveness to this advantage, made effective by a taste for machines and by remarkable mobility. George Wallis, a member of the visiting British Commission of 1853, reported, "Bringing a mind prepared by thorough school discipline . . . the American boy develops rapidly into the skilled artizan . . . he is never content until he has mastered all."[8] He also confirmed Michael Chevalier's 1833 observations that the American conformed "easily to new situations and circumstances; he is always ready to adopt new processes and implements, or to change his occupation. He is a mechanic by nature."[9] Americans moved frequently from job to job, even within a single establishment. This prevented them from developing the highest levels of skill but gave them understanding of ranges of related operations that encouraged inventiveness and improvement.

Even those most conscious of the imperative need for the mechanic's fingertip knowledge were anxious to rest this talent upon principle. Franklin, within the same context in which he urged instruction in drawing to develop the mechanic's spatial thinking, urged education in "Principles" or science. "How many Mills are built and Machines constructed," he asked, "at great and fruitless Expence, which a little Knowledge in the Principles of Mechanics would have prevented?"[10]

The concept of machine technology as "applied science" was accepted with hardly any demur by scientists, mechanics, and the public at large. The better mechanics all went hopefully to books, to scientists, and to scientific institutions for aid as the cases of Fitch, Rumsey, Fulton, and Morse amply document. Oliver Evans emphasized forcefully the aid he received from one professor in the University of Pennsylvania and from experiments "found in scientific works." He urged the government to employ the ingenious in carrying through scientific experiments designed to provide the information required for machine development. Moreover, the belief that technology should rest upon science and principle was taken for accomplished fact in the popular imagination, spurred on by a revival of Baconianism. The *Scientific American* habitually presented steamboats, canals, and manufactures as "the results of . . . science reduced to practice."[11]

The American leaders in the professionalization of science from the 1820s to the 1850s also insisted that science not merely should but did undergird technological advance, and they were anxious to increase that beneficent influence. Alexander Dallas Bache carried the Franklin Institute's committee on inventions to a new level of responsibility in reviewing inventions, and he led the institute's steam boiler explosion inquiry, the first scientific study of this sort. Joseph Henry was governed by his belief that science could predict which inventions would work and which, in a given "state of the art," would not. Much as Franklin had reacted to wrongly designed mills, he reacted to the rows of useless invention models at the Patent Office—mistakes he was confident could have been prevented by science.[12]

"Men of science" were anxious to have their work used to aid technological advance and national improvement but generally shrank from such "contests" with the world, and nearly all resented being ranked beside inventors and projectors.[13] Their view of the character of technological creativity and of the technology-science relationship was artificial. The best dreams of men of the day about new realms of technology that new scientific knowledge would make possible have been far exceeded, but they were wrong in seeing technology as a mere derivation of science.

In the sense of man's ability to manipulate his physical world—without being able to analyze the causes and effects involved—technology long antedated science. Yet the two were often concerned with the same phenomena and required the same spatial perception of multiple, related actions. Science had flourished by what has been labeled "reductionism," by separating from complex phenomena limited events, the causes and effects of which could be numbered, measured, and subjected to logical analysis. The men of science of the nineteenth century in their effort to understand the three-dimensional world drew upon a long and rich tradition of scholarship, not merely upon mathematics and newly emphasized techniques of experimentation, but inescapably upon the sequential, linear logic derived through man's greatest invention: verbal language. Much of the strength of science depended upon precisely this combination of spatial perception and contemplation with numeration and verbalized abstractions.

But there was nothing abstract about a machine, and the scientific principles derived by the early nineteenth century described only the smaller part of the elements and processes required to put together a working machine. In fact, even today scientific principles are no more than important data used by the machine builder; science does not determine the specific components and their arrangement in any machine. The most essential process in designing a workable steamboat and telegraph would not have been significantly altered if the Carnot Cycle had already been enunciated, and Ohm's and Kirchhoff's laws clearly known.

Designing a machine is a creative process. Scientific laws and experimental, analytical data had increasingly to be fed into the process, to become a part of the design along with physical components, linkages, and arrangements. The composition can be achieved only by an exercise in spatial thinking, and this kind of thinking differs markedly from verbal thinking. Design means thinking out plans for accomplishing actions that always permit alternative combinations. There is no deterministic or scientific way to design a machine.

Only recently has the special mode of thinking required in mechanical technology come to attention. Eugene S. Ferguson points out that "Many features and qualities of the objects that a technologist thinks about cannot be reduced to unambiguous verbal descriptions; they are dealt with in his mind by a visual, non-verbal process. . . . The designer and the inventor who bring elements together in new combinations, are each able to assemble and manipulate in their minds devices that as yet do not exist."[14] Anthony F. C. Wallace insists that the work of the mechanic is "in large part, intellectual work . . . [a] kind of thinking . . . unlike that of linguistic or mathematical thinking . . . [but] in no way inferior. In this mode of cognition, language is auxiliary."[15]

The overwhelming truth of such observations strikes the modern ear as new only because it has been so obscured by traditional education. Classical education, as formalized for example in the seven liberal arts, was based upon verbal language and sequential thinking. The trivium, or initial barrier, of grammar, rhetoric, and logic, was entirely a matter of using and thinking in verbal language. The quadrivium moved beyond: arithmetic was another linear language, but music, geometry, and astronomy have both verbal-linear and spatial characteristics. Note, for example, that geometry might seem a prototypical spatial study, but the manner in which it was approached—through the logical manipulation of axioms, corollaries, propositions, and lemmas—was wholly verbal. The three R's of course merely democratized the verbal-linear barrier.

Men close to machine technology always understood the inadequacy and even irrelevance of words and numbers. So long as the mechanical crafts were transmitted at their own pace, apprentices could be adequately indoctrinated in the required skills, "feel," and spatial thinking. Some educators understood and even tried to apply the approach more broadly. In the seventeenth century, Comenius recognized that "Mechanics do not begin by drumming rules into their apprentices" but show them the work "they wish them to imitate," and elements of his influence persisted. More specifically, the eighteenth-century Swedish engineer, Christopher Polhem, invented what he called a "mechanical alphabet" as part of his effort to speed the industrialization of his country. He identified and rendered in the form of a group of wooden models a number of mechanical actions that formed the components of most mechanisms: gears and gear couplings, ratchets, linkages, cams, and drive shafts. His intention was to fill the minds of students with visual and tactile images of the components of mechanisms so they could then manipulate them mentally as they designed machines.[16]

Gaspard Monge's development of descriptive geometry and of improved approaches to engineering drawing was related to his efforts to forward French industrialization following the Revolution. His colleagues, Jean Hachette, Philippe Louis Lanz, and Augustin de Betancourt, classified elementary mechanisms and published drawings of them in tabular form. This was carried to unproductive lengths when Charles Babbage tried to devise a grammar of machines, but alphabets or tables of elementary mechanisms became an accepted part of the instructional approach. Jacob Bigelow, for example, who tried to apply science to technology at Harvard, published his own classified "Elements of Machinery" with copious illustrations. Munn and Company, who took over the publication of the *Scientific American* and became the leading patent firm, regularly published lengthy tabulated drawings of "Mechanical Movements" to encourage inventors and to recruit customers.[17]

Robert Fulton reflected this understanding remarkably well. "The mechanic," he wrote, "should sit down among levers, screws, wedges, wheels, etc. like a poet among the letters of the alphabet, considering them as the exhibition of his thoughts, in which a new arrangement transmits a new Idea to the world."[18]

It becomes clearer how artists, used to filling their minds with the images they struggled to express on canvas, might understand the process of filling their minds with mechanisms in order to design machines. Fulton and Morse were far from unique, merely the most successful. Behind them directly stood Thornton and Latrobe and a little further back, as a decorative artist, Fitch. Both Charles Willson Peale and his son Rembrandt were effective artists and active, inventive mechanics who contributed to several fields of technology. Joshua Shaw painted in Philadelphia but returned to England where he took up inventing percussion cartridges and gun lock improvements. Ithiel Town, inventor of the Town bridge truss, was one of several architects who contributed directly to technology. Rufus

Porter was a landscapist and muralist, rather primitive in his style, who also invented machines and launched the most successful magazine of invention and mechanism, the *Scientific American*.

Morse defined design as he applied the word to the title of the National Academy and to his professorship at New York University, but William Dunlap carried his distinction between verbal and spatial a step further. He wrote, "Poetry, as we are told, excites images and sensations through the medium of *successive action*, communicated by sounds and *time*. The same may be said of music; but painting and her sister *arts of design* rely upon *form* displayed in *space*." Associating these spatial arts with technology, an 1853 announcement of work in the Arts of Design at New York University specifically noted its applicability to "the Mechanic arts."[19]

Morse's travel notebooks show ships, lamps, and axes as well as conventional landscapes. They also picture component elements he sought out to be incorporated in projected paintings—in just the way he sketched telegraph components in his 1832 notebook. The mix, after a time, came easy to Morse, producing a peculiarly mixed and poignant metaphor in a letter to Alfred Vail. "I long," he wrote, "to see the machine . . . you have been maturing in the Studio of your brain."[20]

The concept of design, which was so central in Morse's thinking, describes remarkably well the creative process in spatial arts and in mechanical technology. Edwin T. Layton has identified design as the essential characteristic of the work of the engineer. He points out that engineers assume technology to have a common denominator, despite its diversity, and that this common denominator is "design" or "ability to design." As he puts it, "design . . . I take to be the central purpose of technology. The first stages of design involve a conception in a person's mind which, by degrees, is translated into a detailed plan or design. . . . Design involves a structure or pattern, a particular combination of details or component parts, and it is precisely the gestalt or pattern that is of the essence for the designer."[21]

Early engineering education was torn by the question of whether verbal, mathematical, and scientific training should be offered first within a school context, or following a period of shop practice and exercises in spatial thinking and doing. There was no question by the mid-nineteenth century that both experiences were needed. Ultimately, the professionalization of engineering identified the engineering societies as the qualifying agencies, and they agreed that "design" was the key requirement. Typically, certification identifies the engineer as "qualified to design."[22]

The essence of design is elusive, but it is never fully subject to logic or rule. Both in the arts of design and in mechanical technology, it is to some degree, as David Pye writes, a "matter of trial and error." The thing designed according to assumptions applied first in mental manipulations has to be produced in order to be tested, and then it has to be modified until it "looks" or "works" right. Design may indeed be a matter of eliminating "misfit" or of attaining the most satisfying "fit."[23]

The spatial thinking relied upon overwhelmingly by artists and predominantly by mechanics and engineers, and its differentiation from the sequential, verbal, logical thinking of the schools has recently been provided with exciting experimental verification. Studies of brain physiology and function have identified two modes of thinking or information processing, each predominantly localized to one of the hemispheres of the brain. Conclusions based upon different methods of inquiry agree that the left hemisphere is specialized to process sequential information—such as speech, arithmetic, and chronological inputs. On the other hand, the right hemisphere is the primary seat for simultaneous inputs: visual, auditory, and tactile; its mode underlies relational perception and orientation in space. The left hemisphere, then, deals best with language, analysis, logic, arithmetic, algebra, time series, and cause-effect relationships; the right hemisphere with interrelated patterns and systems, synthesis, spatial and field problems, and, of course, design. Moreover, there is indication that some problems may be solved by either hemisphere, but that similar answers are attained by very different processes.[24]

The classic experiments which first began to reveal this brain function were performed in the 1960s by Roger W. Sperry using a group of subjects whose *corpus callosum*, connecting the two hemispheres, had been severed as a therapeutic measure, successful in combating severe epileptic seizures. Inputs and outputs were then possible from each isolated hemisphere, and the function of each could be tested. Since then, the basic results have been confirmed by other approaches. Subjects with damage to, or surgical removal of, portions of one hemisphere have been studied. More important, normal subjects yielded similar results when comparative reaction times were measured to inquiries targeted to one hemisphere or when the differential electrical activity of the two hemispheres was compared.[25]

The picture is still far from clear. Two modes of thinking are indicated but some experimenters believe that additional modes are possible. The degree of localization is unknown; even given two clear modes of thought, the extent to which each habitually interpenetrates the other is unclear. Under any circumstances, the normal brain is an integrated brain, and those who have pictured successful scientists as left-brain specialists and successful artists as right-brain specialists are egregiously wrong.[26] Yet bimodal thinking within the integrated brain is a reality evident in the historical record and now confirmed in current neurophysiological studies.

The use of the spatial mode of thinking, effectively supported by analytical, logical thought, is of course fundamental in technological development in all countries, in all periods. Why, however, did it flourish especially in the United States in its early decades? Why did a country less culturally developed and less wealthy than the nations of Western Europe assume leadership in certain lines of invention and innovation?

A part of the answer is simply that there was so much to be done. From the very beginning, men had been conscious of the vast riches and the unexampled opportunity offered by the undeveloped continent. Yet even the early population centers were separated by large distances, centers of production were sometimes almost isolated, and there were so few hands to convert all the potentials into a better way of life. Drive and imagination were automatically encouraged. Perceptive visitors were not surprised to find "the spirit of enterprise". . . "the distinctive characteristic of the American."[27] The cultural and

religious heritage had combined with two centuries of experience to impress upon Americans the social and personal
benefits effective effort might yield. There were only spotty
reflections here of the machine breaking experienced in England. The new technology was resisted in some communities
and on some occasions, but more often it enjoyed resounding
support. Most evident was a new life to be won—not an old
one to be defended.[28]

The Americans were fortunately free of many of the constrictions of the Old World. They had not transferred all of
them and the manner in which the American Revolution was
used to eliminate others is familiar, especially in the political,
religious, and social dimensions of life. Yet much of the
American advantage was a function of its undeveloped, rather
than underdeveloped, state. Mancur Olson has recently pointed
to the almost unavoidable progression in any long-established
society toward increased constriction and rigidity in its economic and institutional structures.[29] The Americans had, indeed, a functioning and commercial economy, but the beckoning opportunity indicated something very much more.
Patterns could more easily be altered because they were less
rigid; sometimes new institutions could be built, new paths
followed without demolishing any preceding structure at all.
The abundant life that Franklin, Washington, and Jefferson
saw ahead required eagerly embraced changes: new ways of
doing things, new institutions, and even multitudes of people
who were not yet here.

Among other effects, the lower level of rigidities in commercial life speeded the developments in managerial effectiveness and control about which business historians have been
increasingly persuasive. Alfred D. Chandler, Jr., in *The Visible
Hand*, places the rise of modern business management in the
1840s, but Thomas C. Cochran sees much earlier roots in
improved accounting systems and in the acceptance of
mechanization.[30]

For the desired mechanization, the Industrial Revolution
had, miraculously, provided tools for the job. These were
received in the United States in a very different spirit from the
manner in which both English mechanics and English entre-

preneurs viewed them. Britain had led in the classical period of mechanization, in part because she had fewer constrictions than the Continent, but by comparison the United States was far more fortunate and the differences showed in attitude. English workers frequently opposed the introduction of "laborsaving" machinery in fear that the manufacturers consciously intended to dispense with their labor. Andrew Ure, philosopher for the manufacturers, urged that and more. He favored laborsaving machinery because it would cut labor costs and, in addition, would replace intractable workmen by reliable machines.[31]

By contrast, American workers generally welcomed laborsaving machines as much as the manufacturers. Economic historians have had a lot of fun discussing whether labor was scarcer in the United States than in England, whether there was a differential scarcity of unskilled versus skilled labor, and whether the scarcity of capital was less or greater than the scarcity of labor.[32] However, in antebellum technology generally, as in the case of the steamboat and telegraph, laborsaving machinery was not conspicuously applied for the purpose or with the result of firing workers. In an old enterprise, it was often introduced to increase production, and in new enterprises, whenever the machines could be afforded and new hands could be found. The Americans used laborsaving machines to do things they could not do without them. Paul Uselding has concluded that factor substitution, that is capital investment in machines to replace wage labor, did not occur until 1850, probably not until the mid-1850s.[33]

A parliamentary committee was told, "In America they might set to work to invent a new machine, and all the workmen in the establishment would . . . if possible, lend a helping hand. . . . But in England. . . . If the workmen could do anything to make a machine go wrong they would do it." Another observer reported, "'there is not a working boy of average ability in the New England States . . . who has not an idea of some mechanical invention or improvement . . . , by which, in good time, he hopes to better his position, or rise to fortune and social distinction.'" A Franklin Institute fair was advised that the American might make "a horseshoe nail more slowly than his

European grandfather . . . but he is thinking out a machine, which will make it for him twice as well and a hundred times faster."[34]

The American eagerness for mechanization became almost palpable. The lack of constriction, or what W. Northcote Parkinson has called "injellititus," was certainly a factor in reducing resistance to change, but the whole American experience has to be called in to account for the enthusiasm.[35] The great hopes and the depressions of the steamboat and telegraph promoters, for example, can be chronicled more easily than explained. They were, however, distinctly typical of the times.

Without almost unquenchable enthusiasm, none of the projectors of inventions could have accomplished what they did; Fitch put his finger on a key quality when he sometimes called his last, unfinished boat, the *Perseverance*. Yet a part of their trouble was their misunderstanding of the process of designing machines or mechanical systems. They, like their society, accepted the concept of an invention as a creative idea, quickly conceived, and deserving of recognition and support from that point on. In fact, the conversion of such an idea into a working machine called for continuing inventiveness and both synthetic and analytic thinking; it embraced much the larger part of the effort. The prevailing view of invention had some validity when applied to a simple action such as cranks and paddles or the portrule. It had very little when applied to a mechanical system such as the steamboat or a combined mechanical and electrical system such as the telegraph. The projectors of those devices had no realization that they were involved in systems design and development, but this, indeed, is what they were doing.

A steamboat was a working system comprising boat, engine, boiler, propulsive mechanism, and linkages, and a telegraph: transmitter, receiver, battery, wires, and wire support or insulating devices. There were several alternative ways of designing every one of the components, and the adoption of any one affected the effectiveness of the others in the system. No single design was *the* steamboat or *the* telegraph, and none was "best" under all circumstances.

The kind of spatial thinking required to conceive a new

boiler or an electric relay was just as essential in conceiving the best "fit" of components, all working simultaneously in an operating system. Such thinking was in no way antithetical to science which had provided and continued to find "principles" and understanding that, in one sense, became additional components within the design. Spatial thinking was the key used in designing the larger systems of which the steamboat and telegraph were themselves components: the boat, river, wharves, available trade, competition, and monopoly protection—or: the telegraph, pricing and operating conditions, available traffic, competition, and monopoly protection. In designing the larger system, Fulton was obviously superior to Fitch and Rumsey, and Morse even more successful.

All of these design and development functions—of a machine component, of a machine system, and of the larger system of which the machine was a part—depended upon a mode of thinking too little regarded because of our great emphasis upon verbal, analytical, arithmetic thought. The arts of design, as Morse defined them, rest most heavily upon spatial, visual, holistic thinking. This mode of thinking is also essential in science, but science has attained its great success by combining it integrally with the sequential, logical, arithmetic mode. Because early-nineteenth-century mechanical technology rested so much more heavily upon spatial thinking than upon analytical, arithmetic thought, it was more related to the arts of design than to science.

Emulation is a concept that grew out of the traditional ways of instructing and working in the useful arts and in the fine arts. It relied almost wholly upon spatial thinking: words and numbers were distinctly auxiliary. Because it focused upon the best models of machines and of the men who made them— instead of upon the problems and needs—it emphasized the positive. The institutions and attitudes that supported emulation were specific to their time, but that concept embraced an enduring insight: mechanical technology has to rest upon effective spatial thinking.

NOTES

CHAPTER 1

1. Frances Honour, *The State of the Industrial Revolution in 1776* (New York, 1977), 54, 86.

2. Adam Smith, *An Inquiry into the Nature and Causes of the Wealth of Nations* [1st ed., 1776] (New York, 1937), 9.

3. This is rather more extended than reduced in Leo Marx, *The Machine in the Garden: Technology and the Pastoral Ideal in America* (New York, 1964).

4. Charles E. Peterson, "Early Lumbering: A Pictorial Essay," in Brooke Hindle, ed., *America's Wooden Age* (Tarrytown, N.Y., 1975), 66; Thomas J. Wertenbaker, *The Planters of Colonial Virginia* (Princeton, N.J., 1922), 15; Charles M. Andrews, *The Colonial Period of American History* (New Haven, Conn., 1934), I, 126, 126n.

5. See especially Samuel Y. Edgerton, *The Renaissance Rediscovery of Linear Perspective* (New York, 1975).

6. Georgius Agricola, *De Re Metallica* [1st ed., 1556], trans. Herbert C. and Lou Henry Hoover (London, 1912).

7. Jacques Besson, *Theatrum Instrumentorum et Machinarum* [1st ed., 1569] (Lyons, 1578); Agostino Ramelli, [*Le Diverse et Artificiose Machine* (Paris, 1588)], trans. and ed. as *The Various and Ingenious Machines* by Eugene S. Ferguson and Martha T. Gnudi (New York, 1978); Jacob Leupold, *Theatrum Machinarum* (10 vols.; Leipzig, 1724–39).

8. Cited by Eugene S. Ferguson in Ramelli, *Various . . . Machines*, 39.

9. William Barclay Parsons, *Engineers and Engineering in the Renaissance* [1st ed., 1939] (Cambridge, Mass., 1967), 106; Fernand Braudel, *Capitalism and Material Life, 1400–1800* [1st ed., 1967] (New York, 1973), 298.

10. Note, for example, Ruth Susswein Gottesman, *The Arts and Crafts in New York, 1726–1776* (New York, 1938), passim; Alfred Coxe Prime, *The Arts & Crafts in Philadelphia, 1721–1785* (Topsfield, Mass., 1929), passim; George Francis Dow, *The Arts & Crafts in New England, 1704–1775 (Topsfield, Mass., 1927), passim.*

11. Charles Howell and Allan Keller, *The Mill at Philipsburg Manor Upper Mills and a Brief History of Milling* (Tarrytown, N.Y., 1979), 52, 62, 117, 124; Arthur Cecil Bining, *Pennsylvania Iron Manufacture in the Eighteenth Century* (Philadelphia, 1938), 79–92.

12. Thomas Ewbank, *A Descriptive and Historical Account of Hydraulic and Other Machines for Raising Water* (New York, 1841), 262–63, 344–45; Henry

J. Kauffman, *The Pennsylvania-Kentucky Rifle* (New York, 1960), 1–23; Penrose J. Hoopes, *Shop Records of Daniel Burnap, Clockmaker* (Hartford, 1958), 95–104; Brooke Hindle, *David Rittenhouse* (Princeton, 1964), 27–40.

13. Brooke Hindle, *The Meaning of the Bethlehem Waterworks* (Bethlehem, 1977).

14. Peterson, "Early Lumbering," 64, 66; Charles F. Carroll, *The Timber Economy of Puritan New England* (Providence, 1973), 63–67, 70–71.

15. Peterson, ibid., 64; Zachariah Allen, *Sketches of the State of the Useful Arts, and of Society, Scenery, etc., etc., in Great-Britain, and Holland, or the Practical Tourist* (Hartford, 1835), I, 159.

16. John U. Nef, *The Conquest of the Material World* (Chicago, 1964), 220–21.

17. J. R. Harris, *Industry and Technology in the Eighteenth Century: Britain and France* (Birmingham, 1971), 4, 6, 8; Nef, ibid., 149.

18. Harris, ibid., 17.

19. D. S. L. Cardwell, *Technology, Science and History* (London, 1972), 66–72.

20. Carroll W. Pursell, Jr., *Early Stationary Steam Engines in America: A Study in the Immigration of a Technology* (Washington, 1969), 5–9.

21. *The Papers of Benjamin Franklin*, ed. Leonard W. Labaree, Whitfield J. Bell, Jr., et al. (New Haven, 1961), IV, 229, 231, 233.

22. Cited from Nathaniel Ames, *Astronomical Diary* [1758], in Max Savelle, *Seeds of Liberty: The Genesis of the American Mind* (New York, 1948), 575.

23. Douglass Adair, *Fame and the Founding Fathers*, ed. Trevor Colbourn (New York, 1974), 246, 14.

24. Francis Bacon, *Novum Organum* [1st ed., 1620], ed. Fulton H. Anderson as *The New Organon* (New York, 1960), xxxv.

25. See Paolo Rossi, *Philosophy, Technology, and the Arts in the Early Modern Era* (New York, 1970), 125; Carlo Cipolla, *Clocks and Culture, 1300–1700* (New York, 1967), 34–36.

26. Francis Bacon, *The Advancement of Learning* [1st ed., 1605] (London, 1951), 106.

27. Ibid., 84–86; Walter E. Houghton, Jr., "The History of Trades," *Journal of the History of Ideas*, 2 (1941), 33.

28. Smith, *Wealth of Nations*, 343.

29. Ibid., 732, 717.

30. The pervasiveness of the concept of emulation is indicated in Shakespeare's varied use of the term: *As You Like It*, IV, i, 10–11; *Richard III*, II, iii, 25; *Troilus and Cressida*, I, iii, 134. Thomas Barton applied to David Rittenhouse one of his passages. William Barton, *Memoirs of the Life of David Rittenhouse* (Philadelphia, 1813), 233.

31. Benjamin Franklin, "Proposals relating to the Education of Youth" [1749], *The Papers of Benjamin Franklin*, ed. Leonard W. Labaree et al. (New Haven, 1961), III, 418n., 418.

32. Ibid., 404n., 418.

33. Benjamin Franklin, "Autobiography," *The Writings of Benjamin Franklin*, ed. Albert Henry Smyth (New York, 1905), I, 241–42.

34. Indeed, one of the many societies established on the model of the Society of Arts was named the Société Libre d'Emulation, Paris, 1776. Roger Hahn, *The Anatomy of a Scientific Institution: The Paris Academy of Sciences, 1666–1803* (Berkeley, 1971), 110; Shelby T. McCloy, *French Inventions of the Eighteenth Century* (Lexington, Ky., 1952), 181.

35. Sir Henry Trueman Wood, *A History of the Royal Society of Arts* (London, 1913), 19; Derek Hudson and Kenneth W. Luckhurst, *The Royal Society of Arts, 1754–1954* (London, 1954), 34; *Premiums by the Society, Established at London for the Encouragement of Arts, Manufactures, and Commerce* (London, 1758).

36. Ibid., 25–28; Wood, *History*, 92; Jared Eliot, *An Essay on the Invention, or Art of Making Good, if not the Best Iron from Black Sea Sand* (New York, 1762).

37. Brooke Hindle, "The Underside of the Learned Society in New York, 1754–1854," in Alexandra Oleson and Sanborn C. Brown, ed., *The Pursuit of Knowledge in the Early American Republic* (Baltimore, 1976), 86–92.

38. William Shipley, [On the Society of Arts], *Gentleman's Magazine*, 26 (1756), 61–62; Hudson and Luckhurst, *Royal Society of Arts*, 39.

39. Worthington C. Ford, ed., *Journals of the Continental Congress, 1744–1789* (Washington, 1906), IV, 224; John Adams, "Discourses on Davila," *The Works of John Adams*, ed. Charles Francis Adams [1850] (Freeport, N.Y., 1977), 233, 246, 267, 279.

40. Brooke Hindle, *The Pursuit of Science in Revolutionary America* (Chapel Hill, N.C., 1956), 268–70; Minutes of the New York Manufacturing Society, 20, 46, New-York Historical Society.

41. Hindle, *Pursuit*, 371–72, 375.

42. Max Farrand, ed., *The Records of the Federal Convention of 1787*, rev. ed. (New Haven, 1966), II, 334, 335.

43. Ibid., 321, 324, 324n.

44. Hudson and Luckhurst, *Royal Society of Arts*, 223.

45. Stacy V. Jones, *The Patent Office* (New York, 1971), 3.

46. Henry Steele Commager, ed., *Documents of American History* (New York, 1947), 141.

47. *The Writings of George Washington*, ed. John C. Fitzpatrick (Washington, 1939), XXX, 493–94.

48. *Congress of the United States: at the Second Session . . . An Act to promote the Progress of useful Arts* [New York, 1790], n.p.

49. P. J. Federico, "The Operation of the Patent Act of 1790," *Journal of the Patent Office Society*, 18 (1936), 237.

50. *Letters of Benjamin Rush*, ed. L. H. Butterfield (Princeton, 1951), I, 74, 492.

51. Commager, *Documents*, 141.

52. "Tench Coxe's Draft," *The Papers of Alexander Hamilton*, ed. Harold C. Syrett (New York, 1966), X, 15–23; "Hamilton's Final Version," ibid., 230–340.

53. Ibid., X, 298–304, 308; Jacob E. Cooke, *Tench Coxe and the Early Republic* (Chapel Hill, N.C., 1978), 182–89.

54. *Writings of Washington*, XXX, 293.

CHAPTER 2

1. "List of Patentees, February 22, 1805," *The New American State Papers: Science and Technology* (Wilmington, Del., 1973), IV, 25.

2. John Fitch, *The Autobiography*, ed. Frank D. Prager (Philadelphia, 1976), 178–79.

3. Thomas Savery, *The Miner's Friend* (London, 1698; reprint, 1828); John Harris, "Engine for Rowing Ships," *Lexicon Technicum* (London, 1708), II, n.p.

4. "List of Patentees, February 22, 1805."

5. Hindle, *Pursuit*, 91, 372–73; Hindle, "Underside," 85–87.

6. Benjamin Franklin, "A Letter . . . Containing sundry Maritime Observations," American Philosophical Society, *Transactions*, 2 (1786), 308–9; Daniel Bernoulli, *Hydrodynamica* (Strasbourg, 1738), 293–300; D. Bernoulli, "Recherches sur la manière la plus avantageuse de supléer á l'action du vent sur les grandes vaisseaux," *Recueil du Prèses qui ont remporté les Prix de l'Académie*, 7 (1776), 62–67, 94–98.

7. Franklin, "Maritime Observations," 307–8.

8. Fitch, *Autobiography*, 154, 165–66.

9. Stacy V. Jones, *The Inventor's Patent Handbook* (New York, 1966), 135–36; Floyd L. Vaughan, *The United States Patent System* (Norman, Okla., 1956), 21.

10. Certificate of James Ogilbie, n.d., Fitch Papers, Library of Congress; Fitch, *Autobiography*, 113.

11. Ibid., 39–43, 50–54, 65–66, 103–11.

12. Ibid., 111; Philip L. Phillips, *The Rare Map of the Northwest by John Fitch* (Washington, 1916).

13. Martin (London, 1747), I, pl. 318; Ferguson (London, 1764), 87–91.

14. John Fitch, Surveying Notebook, 1783–84, Fitch Papers, Library of Congress; Fitch to American Philosophical Society, August 1, 1785, ibid.; Fitch to Congress, August 29, 1785, ibid.

15. Henry Voight to William Thornton, n.d., Thornton Papers, Library of Congress; Fitch, untitled and undated drawings, Fitch Papers, Library of Congress.

16. Fitch to Congress, August 29, 1785.

17. Fitch, *Autobiography*, 117n.

18. Fitch to Congress, August 29, 1785; Fitch, *Autobiography*, 154.

19. Ibid., 154, 150–51.

20. Ibid., 156–57; Thornton to Mr. Vining, June 4, 1790, Fitch Papers, Library of Congress.

21. Ella May Turner, *James Rumsey, Pioneer in Steam Navigation* (Scottsdale, Pa., 1930), 30.

22. *Journal of the Continental Congress*, XXIV, 433, 434.

23. Washington to Rumsey, September 7, 1784, *Writings of Washington*, XXVII, 468; Turner, *Rumsey*, 68.

24. Rittenhouse to Thomas Barton, February 3, 1772, Barton, *Memoirs of Rittenhouse*, 231.

25. Englehart Cruse, *The Projector Detected* (Baltimore, 1788), 4–5; J. T. Desaguliers, *A Course of Experimental Philosophy* (London, 1744), II, 467, pl. 36–40; Joseph Barnes, *Remarks on Mr. John Fitch's Reply to Mr. James Rumsey's Pamphlet* (Philadelphia, 1788), 2–16; Turner, *Rumsey*, 81, 91.

26. Fitch, *Autobiography*, 193–97; Fitch, Steamboat History, Library Company of Philadelphia, IV, 298.

27. Fitch, *Autobiography*, 193–94.

28. Thornton to Don Manuel de Soratea, June 1820, Thornton Papers, Library of Congress.

29. Fitch, *Autobiography*, 167; Pursell, *Early Steam Engines*, 34–35, 49–50.

30. Fitch, *Autobiography*, 115–16.
31. William Thornton, *Short Account of the Origin of the Steamboat* (Washington, 1814), 4.
32. Fitch Papers, Library of Congress, passim; Fitch, *Autobiography*, 178–83, 196–200.
33. Ibid., 117n.
34. Whitfield J. Bell, Jr., "William Rumsey," September 29, 1967; American Philosophical Society, Minutes, 3, April 18, 1788.
35. American Philosophical Society, Minutes, 3, December 2, 1785; *Minutes, Tenth Pennsylvania Assembly* (Philadelphia, 1787), 99.
36. James Rumsey, *Explanations and Annexed Plates* (Philadelphia, 1788), pl. 3; Patent Number 1673, November 6, 1788.
37. American Philosophical Society, Minutes, 3, December 2, 1785; James Rumsey, *A Short Treatise on the Application of Steam* (Philadelphia, 1788) [reprinted, E. B. O'Callaghan, ed., *The Documentary History of the State of New York* (Albany, 1849), 1012–38]; John Fitch, *The Original Steamboat Supported* (Philadelphia, 1788); Barnes, *Remarks*.
38. American Philosophical Society, Minutes, 3, April 17, 1789; Rumsey, *Short Treatise*, in O'Callaghan, *Documentary History*, 1038.
39. Rumsey to Washington, May 15, 1788, James A. Padgett, ed., "Letters of James Rumsey," *Maryland Historical Magazine*, 32 (1937), 145.
40. Franklin to Vaughan, May 14, 1788, Turner, *Rumsey*, 142; Jefferson to Vaughan, July 23, 1788, *Papers of Jefferson*, XIII, 394–98; Benjamin Rush to John Coakley Lettsom, May 4, 1788, Thomas J. Pettigrew, *Memoirs of the Life and Writings of the Late John Coakley Lettsom* (London, 1817), 430–31; Thornton to Lettsom, July 26, 1788, ibid., 528, 29.
41. Turner, *Rumsey*, 142–44.
42. Ibid., 144, 152; Rumsey to Franklin, August 10, 1788, Franklin Manuscripts, American Philosophical Society, 36, pt. 1, p. 83.
43. Jefferson to Joseph Willard, March 24, 1789, *Papers of Jefferson*, XIV, 699.
44. Ibid., 198.
45. Rumsey to Levi Hollingsworth, June 30, 1790, American Philosophical Society, Miscellaneous Manuscripts.
46. Fitch, Steamboat History, 233–37.
47. Fitch, *Autobiography*, 207–9; Thompson Westcott, *The Life of John Fitch* (Philadelphia, 1857), 363.
48. Samuel Morey Patent, March 18, 1795, Restored Patents, I, 47, National Archives; Frederick H. Getman, "Samuel Morey," *Osiris*, 1 (1936), 278–302.
49. John Stevens, "Memorial," February 27, 1816, *New American State Papers: Science and Technology*, VI, 124; Archibald Douglas Turnbull, *John Stevens* (New York, 1928), passim, 86.
50. David Read, *Nathan Read* (New York, 1870), 47–51, 101.
51. Latrobe to Robert Patterson, April 19, 1799, American Philosophical Society Archives.
52. Talbot Hamlin, *Benjamin Henry Latrobe* (New York, 1955), 8–17, 27; Lee William Formwalt, "Benjamin Henry Latrobe and the Development of Internal Improvements," Ph.D. diss. (Catholic University, 1977), 5–7.
53. American Philosophical Society, *Transactions*, 6 (1809), 90–91.
54. Pursell, *Early Steam Engines*, 63; Turnbull, *Stevens*, 139; Evans, *Abortion*,

96, 98; Anthony F. C. Wallace and David J. Jeremy, "William Pollard and the Arkwright Patents," *William and Mary Quarterly*, 3d ser., 34 (1977), 420; *Aurora*, March 5, 1804, cited by Greville and Dorothy M. Bathe, *Oliver Evans* (Philadelphia, 1935), 91.

55. Pursell, *Early Steam Engines*, 28–30; Fulton to Latrobe, draft, January 24, 1815, Montagu Collection, New-York Historical Society; Fulton to Roosevelt, October 16, 1815, ibid.

56. Evans, *Abortion*, 22.

57. Ibid., 92–93.

58. Cadwallader David Colden, *The Life of Robert Fulton* (New York, 1817), 144; James Thomas Flexner, *Steamboats Come True* (New York, 1944), 266–67.

59. American Institute Committee Report, June 17, 1845, LeBoeuf Collection, New-York Historical Society.

60. Fulton to Mary Fulton, September 1796, quoted in John S. Morgan, *Robert Fulton* (New York, 1977), 35–36; West quoted in Flexner, *Steamboats*, 220.

61. William Dunlap, *History of the Rise and Progress of the Arts of Design* [1834] (New York, 1965), I, 274; *Scientific American*, 2 (September 26, 1846), 4; Fulton to West, May 22, 1814, LeBoeuf Collection, New-York Historical Society.

62. H. W. Dickinson, *Robert Fulton, Engineer and Artist* (London, 1913), 22; Flexner, *Steamboats*, 118–19.

63. Fulton, *A Treatise on Canal Navigation* (London, 1796), vii, xiii; Dickinson, *Fulton*, 33–35, 37–39.

64. Fulton, *Canal Navigation*, t.p.; Robert H. Thurston, *Robert Fulton* (New York, 1891), 113.

65. Robert Fulton, *Torpedo War and Submarine Explosions* (New York, 1810), 4; Fulton-Livingston Contract, October 10, 1802, in Alice Crary Sutcliffe, *Robert Fulton and the "Clermont"* (New York, 1909), 117–22.

66. William Thornton to Ferdinando Fairfax, draft, December 7, 1814, Thornton Papers, Library of Congress; Robert Fulton, extract of John Fitch Steamboat History, Montagu Collection, New-York Historical Society.

67. Fulton to Fulmer Skipwith, December 12, 1802, LeBoeuf Collection, New-York Historical Society.

68. Flexner, *Steamboats*, 291–92.

69. Robert Francis to George Hammond, June 30, 1804, F.O. 5/44, Public Record Office; William Thornton, Answers for the District Court of Pennsylvania, Third Circuit, n.d., Thornton Papers, Library of Congress.

70. Fulton to Boulton and Watt, September 15, 1810, quoted in Dickinson, *Fulton*, 230–32.

71. Fulton to James Monroe, December 27, 1814, Miscellaneous Manuscripts, New-York Historical Society; List of Patentees, January 1, 1811, *New American State Papers: Science and Technology*, IV, 43; Thornton, *Short Account*, 6–7.

72. Fulton to Lord Stanhope, April 10, 1811, Miscellaneous Manuscripts, New-York Historical Society; Robert Fulton and Edward P. Livingston, *Memorial*, [Albany, 1814], 9–10; Thornton to Fulton, June 16, 1809, Miscellaneous Manuscripts, New-York Historical Society.

73. Stevens, "Memorial," February 27, 1816, 124; Louis C. Hunter, *Steamboats on the Western Rivers* (Cambridge, Mass., 1949), 66–81.

74. Ibid., 122–33; Bruce Sinclair, *Early Research at the Franklin Institute: The Investigation into the Causes of Steam Boiler Explosions* (Philadelphia, 1966); John Burke, "Bursting Boilers and Federal Power," *Technology and Culture,* 7 (1966), 18, 19.

CHAPTER 4

1. Robert E. Gallman, "Gross National Product in the United States, 1834–1909," *Output, Employment, and Productivity in the United States after 1800* (New York, 1966), 4, 23.
2. Morse to Jedediah and Elizabeth Morse, June 7, 1807, *Samuel F. B. Morse: His Letters and Journals,* ed. Edward Lind Morse (Boston, 1914), I, 15; Oliver W. Larkin, *Samuel F. B. Morse and American Democratic Art* (Boston, 1954), 13–17.
3. Ibid., 11.
4. Morse to Jedediah and Elizabeth Morse, June 25, 1810, January 9, 1809, August 1809, *Morse Letters,* I, 21, 18, 19.
5. Morse to Sidney and Richard Morse, February 1811, ibid., 32; Carleton Mabee, *The American Leonardo: A Life of Samuel F. B. Morse* (New York, 1943), 24.
6. Dunlap, *Rise of the Arts of Design,* III, 89–90.
7. Ibid., 90.
8. Morse to Jedediah and Elizabeth Morse, May 3, 1815, January 30, 1812, *Morse Letters,* I, 177, 63.
9. Quoted by Mabee, *American Leonardo,* 48.
10. Dunlap, *Rise of the Arts of Design,* III, 89–90.
11. Mabee, *American Leonardo,* 80–91.
12. Quoted by Samuel I. Prime, *The Life of Samuel F. B. Morse* (New York, 1875), 103; Sidney's reference was certainly to Benjamin Martin, *The Principles of Pump-Work; Illustrated and Applied in the Construction of a New Pump* (London, n.d. [1766]), which described and pictured a double cylinder pump with leather pistons.
13. Augur to Morse, December 9, 1823, Morse Papers, Library of Congress; *Morse Letters,* I, 245.
14. Morse to James E. Lewis, February 17, 1869, Morse Papers, Library of Congress; Morse to Jedediah and Elizabeth Morse, November 18, 1825, ibid.; Morse to Lucretia Walker Morse, August, 27, 1823, *Morse Letters,* I, 249.
15. Morse, "Resolutions," January 14, 1825, ibid., 279–80.
16. Ibid., 279; Thomas S. Cummings, *Historical Annals of the National Academy of Design* (Philadelphia, 1865), 38, 64; Samuel F. B. Morse, *Academies of Arts* (New York, 1827), 30–31.
17. William H. Jones to Morse, April 19, 1828, Morse Papers, Library of Congress; Henry C. Pratt to Morse, April 13, 1828, ibid.; John Neagle to Morse, May 15, 1828, May 25, 1828, ibid.
18. Morse to Jedediah and Elizabeth Morse, November 18, 1825, January 1, 1826, ibid.
19. *Morse Letters,* I, 298–99; Morse to Sidney and Richard Morse, September 21, 1832, ibid., 432.

20. Ibid., II, 25.

21. Ibid., 12, 6.

22. Ibid., 6.

23. Ibid., I, 290.

24. Morse, 1832 Notebook, Smithsonian Institution, passim.

25. Morse, 1837 Portrule, Smithsonian Institution.

26. Morse to Sidney E. Morse, January 23, 1839, in Amos Kendall, *Morse's Patent* (Washington, 1852), 5.

27. Charles T. Jackson, "Notice of the Revolving Electric Magnet of M. Pixii, of Paris," *American Journal of Science*, 24 (1833), 146–49.

28. *Morse Letters*, II, 18, 19, 21, 25.

29. Mabee, *American Leonardo*, 172, 177.

30. *Morse Letters*, II, 38; Theodore F. Jones, *History of New York University* (New York, 1933), 33, 37n., 37, 38.

31. Prime, *Morse*, 246–47; Dunlap, *Arts of Design*, III, 171.

32. *Morse Letters*, II, 42–43.

33. Philip K. Lundeberg, *Samuel Colt's Submarine Battery: The Secret and the Enigma* (Washington, 1974), 22–23; W. James King, *The Development of Electrical Technology* (Washington, 1962), 296; Morse to Levi Woodbury, *Twenty-fifth U.S. Congress, Document #15*, 32.

34. *The Papers of Joseph Henry*, ed. Nathan Reingold et al. (Washington, 1975), II, 90–96.

35. Joseph Henry, "On the Application of the Principle of the Galvanic Multiplier to Electro-magnetic Apparatus," *American Journal of Science*, 19 (1831), 400–408.

36. Bayrd Still, Memorandum to Carl Prince, December 16, 1977, 4a; King, *Electrical Technology*, 297.

37. See illustration, page 118.

38. James D. Reid, *The Telegraph in America* (New York, 1879), 88–89; *Morse Letters*, II, 70; Morse Medal, Smithsonian Institution; "Report of the Committee of Arts and Sciences of the American Institute," September 12, 1842, in Alfred Vail, *The American Electro-Magnetic Telegraph* (Philadelphia, 1845), 88–89.

39. "Report of the Franklin Institute," February 8, 1838, ibid., 79–80.

40. *Morse Letters*, II, 81–82; Mabee, *American Leonardo*, 210–11.

41. Ibid., 225, 216; Morse, "Reply," September 27, 1837, *Twenty-fifth Congress, Document #15*, 28–31; *Morse Letters*, II, 84–86, 92–96, 107–8; King, *Electrical Technology*, 298.

42. Beaumont Newhall, *The Daguerreotype in America* (New York, 1968), 15–18; Donald Fleming, *John William Draper and the Religion of Science* (Philadelphia, 1950), 21–25; Jones, *New York University*, 309.

43. Joseph Henry to Morse, May 6, 1839, *Morse Letters*, II, 140–41; Henry to Morse, February 24, 1842, Vail, *American Telegraph*, 88; Joseph Henry, "Improvement of the Mechanic Arts," *Scientific Writings of Joseph Henry* (Washington, 1886), I, 309–10.

44. Thomas Coulson, *Joseph Henry: His Life and Work* (Princeton, 1950), 215; Arthur P. Molella, "The Electric Motor, the Telegraph, and Joseph Henry's Theory of Technological Progress," *Proceedings of the IEEE*, 64 (1976), 1276; see also Nathan Reingold and Arthur P. Molella, "Theorists

and Ingenious Mechanics: Joseph Henry Defines Science," *Science Studies*, 3 (1973), 323–51.

45. Ibid., 1275; Coulson, *Henry*, 64; *Morse Letters*, II, 261–64.

46. Ibid., 158; Mabee, *American Leonardo*, 248.

47. Ibid., 252–61; Morse to W. W. Boardman, August 10, 1842, *Morse Letters*, II, 74–76; ibid., 198–200.

48. Morse to Susan Morse, November 14, 1838, ibid., 117; Vail, *American Telegraph*, 40–41.

49. Bernard S. Finn, "Telegraph Practice in the Nineteenth Century," paper delivered at 15th International Congress of the History of Science (1977), 1–2.

50. Henry to Morse, May 6, 1839, *Morse Letters*, II, 140–41; Fleming, *Draper*, 40–41; Morse, "Experiments made with one hundred pairs of Grove's Battery," Draper, "On the law of the conducting power of wires," *American Journal of Science*, 45(1843), 390–92, 392–94.

51. Morse to Vail, March 15, 1843, *Morse Letters*, II, 204–5; Morse to Dr. Aycrigg, May 8, 1844, ibid., 221; Mabee, *American Leonardo*, 265–66.

52. *Morse Letters*, II, 209–10, 215–16; Robert C. Post, *Physics, Patents, & Politics: A Biography of Charles Grafton Page* (New York, 1976), 66; Coulson, *Henry*, 216–17; Morse to McClintock Young, June 3, 1844, Vail, *American Telegraph*, 98–101.

53. *Morse Letters*, II, 219, 221–22, 225–26; Mabee, *American Leonardo*, 273–74.

54. Ibid., 282–84; Newhall, *Daguerreotype*, 16.

55. Mabee, *American Leonardo*, 285–87; *Morse Letters*, II, 232.

56. Ibid., 246–47; King, *Electrical Technology*, 300; Prime, *Morse*, 548; Robert L. Thompson, *Wiring a Continent* (Princeton, 1947), 41–69.

57. *Morse Letters*, II, 313; Vail to Morse, December 18, 1840, ibid.; Lundeberg, *Colt's Battery*, 35; Vail, *American Telegraph*, 145–49; Prime, *Morse*, 649–52.

58. King, *Electrical Technology*, 299; Mabee, *American Leonardo*, 287, 315, 355–58; Prime, *Morse*, 630, 671, 699; Moses Beach, *Wealth and Pedigree of the Wealthy Citizens of New York City*, 4th ed. (New York, 1842), 18; *Morse Letters*, II, 390–92.

CHAPTER 6

1. Christian Schussele, *Men of Progress*, 1862, National Portrait Gallery; see p. 125.

2. Nathan Rosenberg and Walter G. Visconti, *The Britannia Bridge* (Cambridge, Mass., 1978), 2.

3. Daniel J. Boorstin, *The Republic of Technology* (New York, 1978), 8–9, emphasizes technology as source of needs rather than response to them.

4. Vaughan, *Patent System*, 19.

5. *Report of the Commissioner of Patents for 1848* (Washington, 1850), 520–22.

6. Willard Phillips, *Law of Patents* (Boston, 1837), 19; *Scientific American*, 8 (November 13, 1852), 69.

7. *Mechanics Magazine*, 6 (1836), 70–72; 7 (1836), iii; American Institute, *Sixth Annual Report, 1848* (New York, 1849), 8–24; William B. Rogers, "A Plan for a Polytechnic School in Boston," in Samuel C. Prescott, *When M.I.T. Was "Boston Tech"* (Cambridge, Mass., 1954), 332; E. G. Sihler, "Names, Mottoes, Symbols in the History of New York University," *New York University Alumnus*, 1 (1920–21), 14, communicated by Bayrd Still.

8. George Wallis, "Special Report," in Nathan Rosenberg, ed., *The American System of Manufactures* (Edinburgh, 1969), 203.

9. Michael Chevalier, *Society, Manners, and Politics in the United States* (Boston, 1839), 285.

10. *Papers of Franklin*, III, 418n.

11. *Scientific American*, 2 (August 21, 1847), 381.

12. Michal McMahon, *Technology in Industrial America* (Wilmington, Del., 1977), xiii–xxiii; Henry, "Improvement of the Mechanic Arts," 309.

13. Nathan Reingold, "Alexander Dallas Bache: Science and Technology in the American Idiom," *Technology and Culture*, 11 (1970), 177.

14. Eugene S. Ferguson, "The Mind's Eye: Nonverbal Thought in Technology," *Science*, 197 (1977), 827.

15. Anthony F. C. Wallace, *Rockdale: The Growth of an American Village in the Early Industrial Revolution* (New York, 1978), 237–38.

16. Frederick B. Artz, *Technical Education in France* (Cambridge, Mass., 1966), 8; *Christopher Polhem*, trans. William A. Johnson (Hartford, Conn., 1963), 38, 157, 158, 182, fig. 31.

17. P. J. Booker, "Gaspard Monge and His Effect on Engineering Drawing," *Newcomen Society Transactions*, 34 (1961–62), 24–31; M. Hachette, *Traité élémentaire des machines* (Paris, 1811); [Philippe Louis] Lanz et [Augustin de] Betancourt, *Essai sur la composition des machines* (Paris, 1808); Charles Babbage, *On the Economy of Manufactures and Machines* (London, 1835); Jacob Bigelow, *The Useful Arts* (Boston, 1840), II, chap. 15.

18. Sutcliffe, *Fulton*, 60.

19. Dunlap, *Arts of Design*, I, 1; Isaac Ferris, untitled printed letter, dated October 1853, Chancellors' Records, New York University Archives, supplied by Bayrd Still.

20. Morse to Vail, October 19, 1837, Vail Papers, Smithsonian Institution Archives.

21. Edwin T. Layton, Jr., "Technology as Knowledge," *Technology and Culture*, 15 (1974), 37.

22. Edwin T. Layton, Jr., *The Revolt of the Engineers* (Cleveland, 1971), 27.

23. David Pye, *The Nature of Design* (New York, 1964), 26; Geoffrey Vickers, "Rationality and Intuition," in Judith Wechsler, ed., *On Aesthetics in Science* (Cambridge, Mass., 1978), 148.

24. Joseph E. Bogen, "Some Educational Implications of Hemispheric Specialization," in M. C. Wittrock et al., *The Human Brain* (Englewood Cliffs, N.J., 1977), 145; Robert W. Ornstein, *The Psychology of Consciousness* (New York, 1972), 39–40, 54; Stuart J. Dimond and J. Graham Beaumont, "Experimental Studies of Hemispheric Function in the Human Brain," in Stuart J. Dimond and J. Graham Beaumont, *Hemispheric Function in the Human Brain* (New York, 1974), 69–71.

25. Roger W. Sperry, "Consciousness, Personal Identity, and the Divided Brain," lecture delivered at the Smithsonian Institution, December 7, 1977,

1–5; H. Hecaen and Martin L. Albert, *Neuropsychology* (New York, 1978), 70–73, 412; Norman Géschwind, "The Anatomical Basis of Hemispheric Differentiation," in Dimond and Beaumont, *Hemispheric Function*, 7–24; Ernest R. Hilgard, *Divided Consciousness* (New York, 1977), 109–10; D. Kimura and Margaret Durnford, "Normal Studies on the Function of the Right Hemisphere," in Dimond and Beaumont, *Hemispheric Function*, 26–44.

26. Joseph W. Meeker, "The Imminent Alliance: New Connections among Art, Science, and Technology," *Technology and Culture*, 19 (1978), 187–98.

27. Guillaume Tell Poussin, *The United States, Its Power and Progress* (Philadelphia, 1851), 486.

28. See Merritt Roe Smith, *Harpers Ferry Armory and the New Technology* (Ithaca, 1977).

29. Mancur Olson, "The Political Economy of Comparative Growth Rates," typescript prepared for conference, 1978, University of Maryland, 17–31.

30. Alfred D. Chandler, Jr., *The Visible Hand: The Managerial Revolution in American Business* (Cambridge, Mass., 1977), 14–16, 75–78; Thomas C. Cochran, "An Analytic View of Early American Business and Industry," Rockefeller Archive Center Conference, October 6, 1978; see also Richard D. Brown, *Modernization: The Transformation of American Life, 1600–1865* (New York, 1976), 128.

31. Andrew Ure, *The Philosophy of Manufacturing* (London, 1835), 19.

32. H. J. Habakkuk, *American and British Technology in the Nineteenth Century* (Cambridge, 1962); Peter Temin, "Labor Scarcity in America," *Journal of Interdisciplinary History*, 1 (1971), 251–64; Paul David, "Labor Scarcity and the Problem of Technological Practice and Progress in Nineteenth-Century America," in *Technological Choice, Innovation, and Economic Growth* (London, 1975), chap. 1; Carville V. Earle and Ronald Hoffman, "The Foundation of the Modern Economy: Agriculture and the Costs of Labor in the United States and England, 1800–1860," *American Historical Review*, 85 (1980), 1055–94.

33. Paul J. Uselding, *Studies in the Technological Development of the American Economy During the First Half of the Nineteenth Century* (New York, 1975), 59.

34. Rosenberg, *American System*, 14, 204; John K. Kane, *Address before the Franklin Institute . . . October 1849* [Philadelphia, 1850].

35. W. Northcote Parkinson, *Parkinson's Law* (Boston, 1957), 78–90.

INDEX

(Illustrations are identified by italics.)